9.11.01

9.11.01

African American Leaders Respond to an American Tragedy

Edited by
Martha Simmons and
Frank A. Thomas

Judson Press
Valley Forge

9.11.01
African American Leaders Respond to an American Tragedy

© 2001 by Judson Press, Valley Forge, PA 19482-0851

Bible quotations in this volume are from the following versions:
The New Testament in Modern English, Rev. Ed. Copyright © J.B. Phillips 1972. Used by permission of The Macmillan Company and Geoffrey Bles, Ltd. (Phillips)
HOLY BIBLE: New International Version, copyright © 1973, 1978, 1984. Used by permission of Zondervan Bible Publishers. (NIV)
The New Revised Standard Version of the Bible, copyright © 1989 by the Division of Christian Education of the National Council of the Churches of Christ in the United States of America. Used by permission. All rights reserved. (NRSV)
The Revised English Bible, copyright © Oxford University Press and Cambridge University Press 1989. (REB)

Library of Congress Cataloging-in-Publication Data

9.11.01 : African American leaders respond to an American tragedy / edited by Martha Simmons, Frank A. Thomas.
      p.   cm.
Includes bibliographical references.
ISBN 0-8170-1435-7 (pbk. : alk. paper)
1. September 11 Terrorist Attacks, 2001–Sermons. 2. Sermons, American–African American authors. 3. Sermons, American–21st century. I. Title: Nine eleven zero·one. II. Title: September eleventh two thousand one. III. Simmons, Martha J. IV. Thomas, Frank A., 1955-

BT736.15 .A13 2001   2001050628
252–dc21

Printed in the U.S.A.
08 07 06 05 04 03 02 01
10 9 8 7 6 5 4 3 2 1

To the memory and ministry
of Rev. Dr. Frederick George Sampson II
"God bless your hearts."

Contents

Introduction
In Times Like These

Martha Simmons

I reside less than a half hour from the airport (Boston-Logan) from which two of the aircraft of terror originated on September 11, 2001. Terror struck more than *close* to home. It struck home. The smoke began to billow, buildings crumbled, and the body count escalated. Words were far too puny to communicate my feelings. This was vast, vast, destruction. Then, for days on end, came the barrage of instant replays of the images of horror.

On the third day after the attack, in a subdued, reflective moment, my thoughts drifted to an old song of the church. A part of it says (and I paraphrase): In times like these, we need a Savior. In times like these, surely our Lord is able. Be very sure, be very sure, your anchor holds and grips the solid rock.[1]

On September 11, 2001, even many who believed that they had a firm hold on the Solid Rock were shaken and startled. Perhaps shaken not so much by the inadequacy of their faith, but by the sheer enormity of the destruction—more than five thousand people killed in one location during the attack in New York alone. Perhaps startled not so much by death, but by yet another example of the depth of evil that still lurks within the hearts of humans.

It is in times like these—painful, petrifying, and perverse times, when we walk around in bewilderment, burdened and brokenhearted—that so many found themselves asking, Is there a word from God? And I asked after September 11, 2001, Who shall bring us a word in times like these?

In times of terror, the African American pulpit has spoken with its clearest voice. Its weighty and lengthy history with attacks is the genesis of its clarity. Perhaps it is also the genesis of its eloquence and passion. Time and again, when evil has spoken, the African American pulpit has also spoken. In all of its diverse forms and diverse faiths, it has spoken. With an unyielding belief in the divine who neither slumbers nor sleeps, it has spoken. With an unwavering belief that right will not always yield to might, it has spoken.

How has it done this? It speaks through four strands that underlie African American preaching. The first is the strand of liberation: "Go tell Pharaoh, let my people go." The second is the strand of providence: "All things work together for good for those who love God." The third is a two-edged strand that focuses us on the "sweet by and by" while bringing us to grips with the sometimes "nasty here and now."[2] The fourth strand embraces and critiques culture, reflecting the *tension* with which persons of African descent who also are Americans daily live.[3]

All of the messages included in this book represent one or more of these strands. Equally important as the strands from which the messages in this book spring, however, is the audience for whom they are written. These messages are written for all Americans and for all citizens of the world. They speak to all of us. They do so by intentionally addressing the issue of terrorism in ways that encompass but also eclipse race. They do so by speaking to experiences that resonate in every house, yes, even in the world-house. They do so through preaching and teaching that provide methods to help us negotiate the maze of terror and remain clothed in our right minds.

The ability to do all of these things comes through centuries of familiarity with intransigent evil. When slavery etched a searing mark on the backs of African Americans and on the landscape of America, the Reverends Harriet Tubman, Richard Allen, Nat Turner, Booker T. Washington, and Jarena Lee all spoke. They proclaimed words of liberation and providence and focused listeners both on heaven and on the here and now.

They did it all as persons of African descent living in tension with being Americans as well.

During the Civil Rights Movement, America's last historical juncture of internal struggle, a new host of African American preachers spoke. There was Martin King Jr., Andrew Young, Ralph Albernathy, and a list of preachers too long to number or name. They stood on the shoulders of Rosa Parks, Vernon Johns, and Benjamin Mays with the same messages as their predecessors, but tuned oratorically for new times.

So, in times like these, with the shadow of 9.11.01 still looming ominously overhead, with bio-terrorism a letter away, and sadness, hatred, and vengeance permeating the national debate, I return to earlier questions: Is there a word from God? And who shall give it in times like these? Is there a word? The response comes from an old spiritual, "Certainly. Certainly. Certainly Lord." Who shall give it? I recommend those who are part of a group that, while not being the only victim of terror's violence, has been and continues to be a target of terror in this nation. Without reservation, I recommend voices from the African American pulpit.

Accordingly, with great honor for attempting such a weighty task, I present these voices of the African American pulpit! They are dynamic pastors and time-honored deans of preaching, some with national and international recognizance; they speak from the academy and they speak in the streets; they represent the post-modern generation and the wisdom of the ages—and each one of them has a message for all of us in times like these. These persons of African descent who are undeniably Americans preach messages about the providence of God for this millennium. They prophesy liberation and accountability for this juncture in history. They offer us a word of encouragement, exhorting perseverance in this troubling time. And, they proclaim a word of peace, challenging us to live looking toward heaven, with our feet firmly planted on earth.

The messages in this book are presented in a manner that is representative of the context in which they were preached or prepared. Material has been condensed or edited only where necessary for publication. Along with the wisdom that can be gleaned from these writers, I trust that as you read, you will also experience the emotions the contributors felt in the "moments" immediately following the tragedy.

Finally, it is my hope in times like these that, as you ponder the words in this book, you will also ponder the words of mystic, theologian, and preacher Howard Thurman:

> At such a time as this, our Father, enveloped by the great quietness instilled by Thy presence, we want to offer the part of us that is clear, unsullied, fresh, clean, untainted, and to hold back under the shadow of our own feelings the things that are tainted and painful and tragic.
>
> Teach us, our Father, how we may be so worthy of our living experience, that we may even now offer to Thee our pain, our suffering, our miseries . . . even as we offer to Thee our best. What a relief it is, O God, to have some place to pour it all out. Our Father, our Father, accept us totally.[4]

In peace.

Martha Simmons
September 2001
Boston, Massachusetts

---

[1]"In Times Like These." Text and music by Ruth Caye Jones. Copyright Singspiration Music, 1944. Reprinted in *The African American Heritage Hymnal* (Chicago, Ill.: Gia Publications, Inc., 2001), 309.

[2]This strand is best understood through a historical analysis of the song "We'll Understand It Better By and By." Text and music by Charles A. Tindley (1905). Reprinted in *The Baptist Standard Hymnal* (Nashville: National Baptist U.S.A. Sunday School Publishing Board,1924), #504.

[3]See the writings of W. E. B. Du Bois for more on the "two-ness" felt by persons of African descent who are also Americans. See especially *The Souls of Black Folk* (New York: The New American Library, 1969), 45.

[4]Howard Thurman, *The Centering Moment* (Richmond, Ind.: Friends United Press, 1980), 59. Copyright 1969 by Howard Thurman. Used by permission of the publisher.

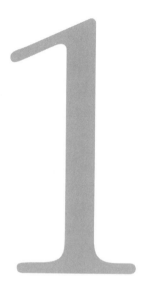

Preach
in Times
Like These

After the Cistern

Gail E. Bowman
September 14, 2001

Found inside a Chinese-American fortune cookie,
kept and remembered:

Happy people rarely correct their faults.

Some of the other preachers here at Dillard and I share
a great respect and admiration
    for the Bible's Book of Beginning, Genesis,
      and its complex and eminently studiable stories
        of people and God.
The humans in Genesis are *really* human and demonstrate
    both how wonderful and how flawed we can be.

Among many favored accounts, to which we continue to return, is
    the story of Joseph, his brothers, his journey, and his life.
You remember Joseph—

    Jacob, Leah, and Rachel had a daughter, several other sons,
        and Joseph, the Dreamer.

But the genealogy is not so important as the relationships.
  The point is that Joseph was favored among *and over* his brothers;
    he was loved, extraordinarily
and, as the Reverend Dr. Jeremiah Wright would say,
"That's where the stuff started."

Many of us remember Joseph as the one who receives from his father
  the gift of a "coat of many colors"
  or, as the New International Version says,
  a "richly ornamented robe."
The robe makes Joseph outstanding, prominent, visible, and
  in a mostly nice way,
    proud.
Some of his siblings, his brothers and sister, can cope with this.
  Joseph is a great guy
    good looking
    dynamic
    young
    extraordinarily able
    with an exuberance that draws and holds every eye.

But other siblings have a problem with Joseph that grows and increases
  with every flash of the gorgeous robe.
Finally, the worst of the siblings formulate a plot to bring Joseph low.
You heard it read,
But let us return and sip again from this particularly bitter
and alienating cup:

  So when Joseph returned to his brothers, they stripped him of his robe
  the richly ornamented robe he was wearing—
  and they took him and threw him into the cistern
  {a well, dry for the moment}.
  When the Midianite merchants came by,
    his brothers pulled Joseph up out of the cistern
    and sold him for twenty shekels of silver
    to the Ishmaelites who took him to Egypt.

In the story of Joseph, this is an especially poignant moment.
Joseph, stripped of his glorious garment, which is then stained
and spotted with blood,
    is shut away from light and human interaction.
    He is left to contemplate the incredible hatred of his brothers,
        a hatred that has been building gradually
        but has clearly taken him unaware.
Surely at this moment, his agonized thoughts are directed toward
his brothers—
    How can they do this?
    How can they hate him so?
    Is his fate completely in their hands?
    Where is God?

Joseph has arrived at a turning point in his life;
    he will not be the same afterward.
What will become of him *after the cistern?*

In the Book of Hosea we are told:
"Take with you words, and go to the Lord."
Many, many in this community are accustomed to doing just this;
    great numbers of us, daily and even by the hour,
        turn to God in prayer.

So it was almost unprecedented Tuesday past
    to come upon a day and a situation so shocking
        that, for a time, we were stripped even of words.
The waves of horror, grief, confusion, worry, and pain hit some of us
almost immediately,
    leaving friends and colleagues asking,
    "Well, do you know someone there?
    Do you have a special connection?"

But as the week progressed, those sorrowful waves have found us all.
Some among us still wait for particular news;
    you ride high on our prayer lists.

And as the specific stories of individuals dribble forth
    we discover it is as we had feared—
    in a strange and unexpected way—
        We know everyone there.
        We have a special connection through the heart and the gut to them all.

Losing that many people from that many places, races, and walks of life
covers any and every ground of familiarity we can name.
    Only a person whose humanity has been burned from them
    as if by secular acid,
    only someone who left their pity behind them so long ago
        that even the faint whispers of it have died from their hearts
            could fail to pause and say:
            "Oh, this is sorrow."
    Even from a bright blue sky, with our spiritual eyes
    we can see the tears of heaven streaming down and down,
    joining and washing in amongst our own.
    Jesus wept. God weeps.

Today, three days later, on this National Day of Prayer and
Remembrance,
    we must recognize that we have just begun our journey
    through the valley of the shadow of death.
Increasingly, the good stories, the miraculous rescues,
    the seemingly arbitrary decisions that saved a life here and a life there
    are behind us,
    and before us stretch sadness and tragedy beyond imagining.
We will find out what we are made of.
We will find out what faith must mean,
    and we will discover, I hope and pray, that human compassion
    knows no limit,

And is, in fact, like the God we serve—so high, you can't get over him,
    so low, you can't get under him,
    so wide, you can't get around him.

We must help; our own humanity is at stake.
We must stand with strangers and, God help us, with friends,
    seeing them through these next days, weeks, and months.
They deserve a piece of our hearts right now,
    as eventually they will require a piece of our hope
    before we can go on, together.

But what of America?
For many of us, every day catches us in the midst of
a love/despair relationship
    with the United States.
Brash and bold,
    alternately profound because of our history
    and wonderful despite it.
On an average day, capable of much of the best and some of the worst
of what humans can be
    we are a great Joseph of a nation—
        Beautiful: oh, go see her, end to end and tip to tip.
        Dynamic: opportunity stirs all of our blood
            and draws the civilized world to us as if to the scent of wine.
        Young: we are still at the beginning of what we can be.
        Extraordinarily able: creative, ambitious, confident,
            we say freedom-loving and freedom-protecting.
        This country has an exuberance that draws and holds every eye.
    No wonder we love her, and no wonder we are proud of her.

But we are also: hated. And we must now come to terms with this.

Seen and experienced from a distance
    and through Hollywood's commercialized and admittedly
    self-serving lens,
        the perception of the United States much of the world holds
        does us few favors.
But a closer and first-hand look at us through the eyes of a needy world
    is not a great deal better.

We are an extraordinarily generous people
  but we are capable of great selfishness also.

  Abundance has taught us to be wasteful.
  Land mass, ocean distances, and vast national resources
    have allowed us to be uncooperative.
  Believing our own press has invited us to rewrite the truth,
  and wealth at times makes us think too well of ourselves.

YET,
All of the kinds of talent and depth that the world possesses have been
assembled in this country.
By the movement of the divine hand and through unspeakable acts
redeemed by grace
  we are all here—

  from the world's religions: Christians, Muslims, Jews,
  Buddhists, Hindus, and more
  from the world's races: blacks and whites, Asians, Latinos,
  Native Americans,
    and all manner of exotic mixes, underrepresented peoples
      And the previously unheard from.
  From the world's great work: business people, artists, scientists,
  social scientists and medical professionals, writers, teachers,
  religious professionals, clerks, service providers, housekeepers,
  athletes, cooks, students, entertainers, carpenters, military people,
  farmers, construction workers, and more
    and a whole group of people who love nothing more
      than serving historically black colleges and universities.
  Here at Dillard, despite our apparent and sometimes visible
  challenges,
    in matters of young women and men claiming their dreams
    through the caring aid and diligent assistance of older men
    and women
          And still we rise.

The United States of America seldom suffers from being too quiet.
Usually, the opposite is true.
We can be loud not only in what we say but what we do.
And loud folks are often not the best listeners,
either to others or themselves.

How long has it been since we seriously examined our national direction
as a whole people?
And when did we last ask God to help in that endeavor?
Well, some of us are asking God now
and we are very welcome, as always, at the foot of the throne.

When Joseph was pulled from the cistern and parted from his brothers,
it was to begin an odyssey of contemplation and maturation.
He never saw his ornamented robe again, but it was the least of his
considerations.

He was in the process of becoming a man—
listening to those around him
allowing others to tell him what they needed
rather than imposing his will upon them
seeing other nations through uncritical and truly interested eyes.

Joseph wasn't a bad person before his trials began,
and in no way did he deserve what happened to him
nor do we
but after the cistern, Joseph was better.
His coat he lost, but the dream he kept.
He turned to God and, in time, he was healed.
Eventually he was able to greet without animosity the brothers
who so wronged him.

It is up to us to determine who we will be after the cistern.
God has not left us; God will not leave us,
we can and will survive the trials ahead.

We have been turned upside down by recent events;
　　we will be fully back on our feet in time.

But the question for us today is
Do we want to return to the same position as before?
　　Or, *Do we want to set our feet on higher ground?*

In recent years American citizens have opted out of full participation
in politics
　　and the obligations of public citizenry.
　　It's time to opt back in.

In recent years we have, as an African American people in particular,
　　accepted too much of the commercial lie.
We've built church real estate instead of helping the community's children
We've put down books and gone to television
　　where we are too often portrayed as helpless parents
　　and clueless individuals.

We used to be Stand Up people, ever alert for human need
　　and always ready to care and share.
The needy, the struggling, were our brothers and sisters.
What have we been doing the past few years?
　　It seems we've been shopping.
At a time when our good sense, gentleness of spirit, and deep sense
of community
　　are desperately needed by our nation,
we've opted out of the value system,
　　the accumulated wisdom, and the heroic and historic dignity
　　of our people.
　　It's time to opt back in.

And some young people in our midst, here, today
　　have started down paths to careers,
　　chosen not through prayer but largely because of income potential.

And we who know better—we who already realize that it's not
the shine of silver
that puts the heart to rest—have let them,
assuming, I suppose, that they are going to find some solace in money
that no other people ever have.
We've opted out of commitments of conscience.
It's time to opt back in.

People have been asking me this week about the national government's
possible response
to these tragic events.
"What," they say, "will *they* do?"

Well, I say the national government is not *them*, it's *us*.
The only reason the national government has gotten in the habit of not
listening for our opinions
is because we've stopped giving them.
It's not *their* government; it's *our* government.
It's not *their* decision; it's *ours*.

An African American female national security advisor
and a president who can quote two lines of the Twenty-third Psalm
do not relieve us of *our responsibility* to consider international options,
participate in national decisions,
and be down on our knees nightly not just in troubled times
but in all times.

So, . . .What does God ask of us today, beloved in the Lord?

First, God asks us not to rush through the process of mourning
and grieving.
A great loss has taken place,
and an incredible immorality has transpired.
God is in his holy temple.
Let all the earth keep silence before him.

Second, God asks us to loosen the strings of our prayer purse
    and slip inside those who planned these deeds,
    those who accomplished these deeds,
    and those who applaud these deeds.
As these monstrous sins come to rest on the back of Jesus,
stretched upon the cross,
    they come to rest beside your sins of yesterday
        and my sins of tomorrow.
They tell me that from heaven, these sins all look and feel the same.

Forgive us our trespasses, O Lord,
As we forgive those who trespass against us.

Jesus asks of us the near impossible, and stands tenderly with us
    among the newly-arrived in glory as we try.
Battle with this, beloved. Battle with this.
And seek God's strength to love.

Third, God asks us be trusting of heaven in the matter of justice.
This spilled blood cries out for justice,
    and eventually, the creaky and imperfect wheels
    of the human justice system must turn.
    But let us remember: True justice, like true vengeance, is God's.

One of the best things about the Joseph story,
    the glimmer of scriptural gold
    that makes all the panning of the assorted details of the
    narrative worthwhile,
        is that at the end, all is made right.
Joseph and his brothers are reconciled.
Our last glimpse finds them in each other's arms.
The brothers look upon the face of their former enemy,
and beg forgiveness of Joseph.
    Joseph grants it readily, saying:
    You intended it for evil but God used it for good.

You intended it for evil, but God used it for good.
What a promise, and what a mighty God we serve!
God specializes in taking evil directed against us
    and using it, in the fullness of time, for good.

In future years, people born in 1999, 2000, 2001 will learn of
these times as a watershed event.
They will turn to us, particularly to you, Class of 2002, Class of 2003,
    Class of 2004, and Jubilee Scholars Class of 2005.
They will say, first,
    "I've studied the record. I know what it was like."
Then you will respond:
    "You can study the record, but you can't know what it was like."

They will speak again, then, saying:
    "It was such an extraordinary experience.
    What changed in your life, what changed in the nation,
        what changed in the world as a result?"

What will you answer?
Oh, what will you say?

    AMEN and AMEN.

An African American Pastoral
on Recent Acts of Terrorism in America

Cain Hope Felder

SEPTEMBER 27, 2001

Since World War II, the American motion picture and television industries have created many imaginary stories about invasions from outer space, the specter of nuclear disaster, asteroids hitting the earth, and kindred scenarios of utter national disaster. These fantasies, often distributed around the world, have made quite a bit of money for media moguls and others. Some of these films more recently have even focused on catastrophes involving the World Trade Center and U.S. government installations such as the Pentagon, the Capitol Building, and the White House.

There was usually enough realism in these products to scare and at the same time entertain people. Few had the slightest thought that such things would actually happen, hurtling us quite suddenly closer to an apocalypse than was thought. On September eleventh, the unthinkable seemed to be occurring as planes were being turned into "flying bombs," causing mass murder along the East Coast of America. Some likened the day's events to the Japanese attack on Pearl Harbor, but these new acts of terrorism somehow seemed more ominous.

Throughout the last half century, the United States of America has evolved into the world's most wealthy, technologically advanced, and militarily powerful leader of the so-called Free World. Her religious institutions—

particularly those of Christianity and Judaism—quietly, during this period, began enjoying unprecedented benefits of what was widely touted as progress in a politico-economic system of free enterprise. The one decade that gave the nation pause was the 1960s, in which the Civil Rights, Anti-Vietnam War, and Feminist Movements seemed to pose serious internal threats to the nation.

Even the church struggled to clarify whether or not its ministry had any stomach for advocating social justice. Indeed, more often than not, the Euro-American church tended to participate in the backlash, domestic accommodations, and co-optations of the 1980s and 1990s. These became effective strategies to calm jitters within the majority culture while the nation returned to a mode of profitability.

By the end of the century, many within America proved that we could have "guns and butter"—guns in the streets and in the suburban homes, butter in the overstocked stores of ever-expanding shopping malls. The overindulgence and pursuit of money would become so frantic that dot-com companies and lotteries took center stage, producing instant millionaires. Not a few Americans even celebrated greed openly, building virtual shrines to selfishness and materialism. One hardly took notice that credit-driven consumerism was becoming a new form of social control.

Few took notice of the dangerous, widening gaps between rich and poor, between the races, or the heightened social pathology within a "pop culture," and the diminishing meaning of religion or the spiritual values intregral to the Bible's vision of "a beloved community." Completely lacking was any real sense of national identity as more and more Americans fused their religiosity with the ideology of capitalism and nationalism. We became far less conscious of our identity as members in the global community than as members of a nation relying more and more on economic indicators, technology, and the police than on God. But, "Black and Blue Tuesday," September eleventh (9-11), changed all of the false security, and our nation suddenly found itself in a bona fide emergency of frightening proportions.

In a sense, white America has been "niggerized," as Cornel West aptly put the matter on the Tom Joyner Morning Show. West made the statement to a large class at Harvard upon his return to Cambridge—having been in New York City. He, of course, was alluding to fact that the black masses in America live on a daily basis with the fear and existential *angst* that comes from being sociopolitical victims of the oppressive racial preference networks in America. "My country 'tis of thee..." Many of us African Americans are often rather intimidated, bullied, and made afraid! Yet, more than this, some of us are frightened for our native land that has so much potential for good and for becoming a stronger beacon of freedom in this unredeemed and merciless world!

By now, the details of the disaster as well as heroic feats and inspiring stories of the day have been well publicized. A nation so ill-affected cannot but invoke the presence of God and cry out in anguish. Nevertheless, many people only invoke the presence of God or adopt the rhetoric and rituals of religion when convenient or in those inevitable times of utter crisis. As a result, our diverse brands of "civil religion" seem more interested in protecting and preserving the church and the socioeconomic status quo than in providing substantive moral leadership that will take more seriously the need for social justice rather than retributive justice. Crisis is also a time for prudence and caution more than an opportunity to wave the nation's flag and to sound the drums of war.

The wiser agenda for survival on the planet is devising a new "foreign policy" based more on genuine altruism rather than politico-economic self-interest. Here, the church could become a model for government efforts in discovering new ways to make friends, not enemies. Our agenda should be to help diverse groups overcome their alienation from other groups. Fear and intolerance of others who seem different have led to hateful acts and great harm. When religion has stood in the background or offered ridiculous commentary, become cleverly opportunistic or relegated itself as mere priests to officiate in ceremonies of mourning, its emptiness becomes glaring.

Sadly, Christianity must free itself more from its Western captivity. In this new millennium, the church—of all stripes—must assist in demonstrating that Christianity, as a religion of sacrifice, love, forgiveness, and empowerment, rises above merely being a mechanism to provide warrants (rewards) or sanctions (threats of punishment) for accommodating the status quo and thereby continuing the cycle of human violence. Indeed, the black church has both a particular burden and a special role to play in ministering to the "soul of a nation." That troubled soul, racked with what Professor Orland Patterson of Harvard has called "the religion of racism," is now exposed for all the world to see at this time of national crisis. Yet blacks are essentially only shadowy figures among the prominent commentators, except for a few select African Americans within the current president's administration or his party.

Instead of seeing its salvation or significance in televangelism, the black church must dust off the tradition of prophetic praxis on behalf of the masses of its people who still languish at the margins or beyond—in prisons, detention centers, and mental hospitals or as the homeless on the streets of America. Some black ministers talk/preach liberation, but most preach and witness in the old narrow vein of Protestant evangelicalism. Far too many focus almost exclusively on personal failings (sin), possible other-worldly benefits (heaven), and the more immediate "this worldly goal" of material prosperity—long structured out of reach for most African Americans. The heyday of the civil rights witness has passed, and the more recent black public witness has been episodic (hate-crime protests, excessive force by the police, the Million Man March, racial profiling, and voter harassment) or symbolic with little sociopolitical impact.

Needed is a new manifestation of African American "Soul Force" wherein blacks would spearhead the formation of interracial and interethnic coalitions for constructive social change on behalf of those groups in America and around the world whose pain we refuse to see and to which there is seldom a meaningful altruistic response. The United States, quick to chauvinism with thinly veiled arrogance, has had extraordinary difficulty responding positively to the pain of others or even hearing their voices of anguish and discontent. Yet, our nation wants—no, demands—that others in the world respond positively to our grief and pain. African Americans are, for example, the most frequent "scapegoat" (Leviticus 16) for the pain of other groups, even certain Arab communities. Despite this, the peculiar status of blacks in America as virtually "native aliens" (Genesis 15:13-14), this may well be the credential necessary for taking the New Testament and Christianity more seriously. What better condition is there for understanding the power of God, the Holy Spirit, and the renouncing of bitterness over the shabby treatment that blacks have received in America for the larger good of establishing a reconciled, "beloved community"? This is precisely what made the public prophetic witness of Rev. Dr. Martin Luther King Jr. so singular.Thus, the horrible events of September eleventh have seared forever in our collective consciousness the simple fact of national vulnerability and terrorism expressed in historic proportions. This is a time for deep reflection and an honest national self-critique based on one simple question: "Why would terrorists want to do such things to America?" It is impossible to answer this question if the participants to the public discussion table are restricted to the majority racial group in America. The answers lie in the foreign policy of the United States, usually perceived in terms of the narrow self-interest of the majority culture.

That policy has too long been one of consistent preference for Europe and Israel, and conversely it has been insensitive to the plight of the Palestinians and persons of African descent, refusing to recognize that, after a while, people who perceive a history of injustice against them will strike back without regard for so-called innocent lives. There was little American, French, or British "hue and cry" or signs of helpful solidarity from America for the genocide in Rwanda and Burundi; there has been only a tepid response to the modern slavery being practiced in parts of the Islamic world (notably Sudan)—nothing that compared to the Western intervention in Serbia and Bosnia.

Americans all are guilty or all are innocent, when perceptions of injustice and violence proceed as matters of national policy. The nation must not be afraid to hear a range of prophetic, dissenting voices (usually absent from or cut off in public debates) that are no less "patriotic" than those of the majority culture. These marginalized voices are informed by years of open bigotry, second-class citizenship, and skewed domestic policies, and such voices must be heard in a nation that construes itself as the capital of the "free world," a true democracy.

One might well ask in all of this, Where is there a higher challenge and call to witness from the church? Are these not times for more than a sentimental pastoral or priestly role for Christianity? Does our understanding of Christianity extend only as far as the national flag? Certainly, the church has multiple roles, particularly ones that seek healing, consolation, and reconciliation, but the church also must be a medium for other constructively critical voices from groups relegated to the margins of society. Such persons have still been largely excluded from the full benefits of the American political economy. They would naturally view socioeconomic and political issues—whether national or global—from different perspectives than the white majority who now call for "national unity."

Yet the deep pain and resentment from groups who routinely see themselves scapegoated, caricaturized, and disenfranchised cannot so easily be dismissed. Experience like the acquittals of police and hate groups who seem instinctively prone to shoot, brutalize, and intimidate blacks with impunity (as in the recent police acquittal in Cincinnati) highlight pervasive and subtle Western racial and cultural "preference networks." Our white brothers and sisters in America can ill afford to ignore or deny the deep injustices that persist in their relations with African Americans, Latinos, and people of color around the globe.

The present moment of crisis is at the same time a moment of opportunity for self-rediscovery and for a more inclusive forum for public debate. The brute exercise of power, whether in the media or in the financial systems of the majority culture, only furthers the cause of terrorism against the nation. We need more wholesome and reconciling approaches to "conflict resolution" and ways to cope with violence than what government officials, Congress, and media executives currently are sending to the youth and children of America. Is our only responsibility to bring them nearer to a global apocalypse? Are African Americans the only ones to be required "to turn the other cheek" and "forgive for righteousness' sake those who persecute" them (Matthew 5)? Are we not making a mockery out of the Martin Luther King Jr. holiday that celebrates the power of nonviolence? Beyond the drum roll, the call to arms, and the heightened rhetoric of retaliation and more violence, lies the vision of Jesus of Nazareth; it is a vision that we all may be of "one heart and soul," of one spirit. To trivialize the contemporary relevance of our Christian faith beyond the parameters of national ideology or apologetics for capitalism is to face the abyss and the increasing possibilities of World War III.

The Gathering of America

T. D. Jakes

SEPTEMBER 16, 2001

We are cognizant of the huge responsibility that rests upon this nation and its leadership and even upon this church to do what we can in some small way to encourage people who are going through adversity. There are many, many people in this church who knew someone or were related to someone who was in the World Trade Center or Washington D.C. when the planes crashed and knew somebody who was on the plane that crashed in Pennsylvania. Hardly any American in this country and few of the friends of Americans around the world have been untouched in some way by the magnitude of the travesty that has occurred before us. I want to talk to you a little bit about that today.

In the Gospel of St. Matthew, chapter 13, beginning with verse 24 (KJV), let us read from the Word of God.

> Another parable put he forth unto them, saying, The kingdom of heaven is likened unto a man which sowed good seed in his field: But while men slept, his enemy came and sowed tares among the wheat, and went his way. But when the blade was sprung up, and brought forth fruit, then appeared the tares also. So the servants of the householder came and said unto him, Sir, didst not thou sow good seed in thy field? from whence then hath it tares? He said unto them, An

enemy hath done this. The servants said unto him, Wilt thou then that we go and gather them up? But he said, Nay; lest while ye gather up the tares, ye root up also the wheat with them. Let both grow together until the harvest: and in the time of harvest I will say to the reapers, Gather ye together first the tares, and bind them in bundles to burn them: but gather the wheat into my barn.

Verse 30 says, "Let both grow together until the harvest: and in the time of harvest I will say to the reapers, Gather ye together first the tares, and bind them in bundles to burn them: but gather the wheat—." Repeat it: But gather the wheat, but gather the wheat into my barn. I want to talk about the gathering of America. The gathering of America.

I stand before you today with mixed emotions. I certainly am, on one hand, glad to be back home and glad to be at the helm of this church to do what God has called me to do. So, it's good to be home. And yet there is a certain sobriety, a certain seriousness, a certain weightiness, that I feel at this moment. I'm weighted not only with the tragedies that have riveted this nation. I'm also weighted with the responsibility of Christian leadership to be used of God to answer questions and to give direction. Significant issues are challenging us. I've been amazed by what has happened in the last few days, not only in terms of what has happened in New York and in Washington, at the Pentagon and what the enemy wanted to do to Air Force One, but also amazed at the open entrée that God has given us to be able to discuss with the nation—through secular media—the impact that these events are having on the nation and the possible medicinal influences that are about in the country when we looked to God for our strength and for our shelter. While we normally have a very, very good crowd, the crowd is stronger than normal [today], and I think that alone reflects your concern and your understanding for the challenges before us.

I want to open by telling you that I have never in the forty-four years of my life seen anything as disturbing as what we've been riveted by in this country at this particular time. Yes, we've had some skirmishes and we've had some Desert Storms and we've gone into Kosovo, and we've thrown some weight around and we've even lost some lives in the process of doing what we thought was appropriate to do, but never in my life, including

Vietnam, have I seen anything that is as disturbing as what I'm seeing occur right now. And if you're taking it seriously, you're a very smart person. If you don't take it seriously, you are very, very foolish. There is a tremendous concern facing this country. Our prayers strongly go out to President Bush. Strongly, strongly. Emphatically. Without question, we're deeply praying for him. And I don't want you to get caught in the trap of you voted for him, you didn't vote for him, you're Republican, you're Democrat, you don't like how the election went. It makes no difference how the election went now. He is the President of the United States of America. Let's be clear.

I believe [President Bush] deserves our whole support, our complete prayer, and our consecration because we have never been threatened like we are being threatened right now. You're hearing words like *campaign;* they're launching a campaign, which is basically just a nice word for *war.* And they're launching a war strategy specifically to protect and defend this country. You're hearing terminology like *a new war.* And one of the reasons that I think we need to bombard the president with prayer is that he's hardly unpacked his office supplies in the Oval Office. He's hardly gotten used to the atmosphere in Washington, D.C. And now he's confronting one of the most serious conflicts in the history of this nation. A conflict that, by the way, is unprecedented. We have nothing to compare it to. Although you've heard a lot of things said about Pearl Harbor, Pearl Harbor is a poor comparison to what we are facing today. More people died in that World Trade Center alone than in all the death and destruction of Pearl Harbor. With one fatal swoop this—this enemy—this evil and wicked, vile person who has moved against us—has turned our own aircraft into bombs that exploded and ignited thousands of lives. The last report I had was 4,972 people have been listed as missing. The numbers are mounting while we're talking. Out of all of that, 152 bodies have been recovered. Ninety-two of them have been identified. Most of the bodies in that rubble are not even recognizable. They are now asking people to bring toothbrushes of their loved ones so that they can test the DNA to be able to identify the bodies that are not recognizable. This is horrendous.

The media has been very tactful and very tasteful in its coverage of this event. They've spared us the gory details. They have not given us close-ups of bodies diving out of windows. They've not given us close-ups of body parts. That's all they've been able to find of people. They have not talked of people who have been set afire and burned. They have not talked about what the heat of jet fuel igniting would do—that it was so strong that it melted steel, that steel lost its strength. The heat force was so strong that people chose to dive out of a window from one hundred and four floors up rather than to face that heat.

Whatever you think this is, it is worse than what you think. But, I think you understand the magnitude of this problem. It's very difficult for me to watch it and see thousands and thousands of people standing up in Manhattan where I had just left a few days before. Walking down the same streets that I had just happened to be on a few days before. Traveling the same airway that I had just happened to travel a few days before. Holding up pictures of loved ones in the hopes that they might find them. Searching the morgues. Searching the hospitals. Desperately waiting. Every time the phone rings, leaping to their feet. Hoping against hope that it might be a call from a loved one. Listening and hoping that some tap or some sound beneath the concrete might be their wives or their mothers or their husbands or their brothers.

This nation is riveted like I have never seen it before. So here we are— in America, from which we have often gone to rescue other countries from these tragedies. It has come home to roost. And we are concerned, we're deeply concerned, and we ought to be concerned. But, the reality is, we can't even begin the comforting process because we've not truly entered into grief yet, because many of us haven't even recognized the magnitude of what happened. And, as that begins to hit this nation and the reality that many of those pictures are going to end up being memorials to people who did not escape....

It is just gut-wrenchingly painful to think of what has happened. There's not a home, an intelligent home in this country that hasn't been riveted by the possibility, that hasn't thought in the back of their mind, That could have been me. That could have happened to us. There's not an intelligent person anywhere in the world who shouldn't understand the vulnerability that has been announced to this country, that everyone is sus- pect. If you've read any papers, you recognize that this is a part of a master and grand scheme that the enemy has unleashed against us, and if anybody ought to be concerned, we ought to be concerned because part of that networking was right here in Fort Worth. So, if you're not going to get concerned with that in your backyard, I don't know who is going to be concerned. If that doesn't drive you to your knees, if that doesn't put you in the position of prayer, shame on you. Because we're not just talking about going somewhere to battle, we're talking about the battle coming to us.

Are you hearing what I'm saying? And so I'm weighted by that! I'm deeply concerned about that and I challenge you to be concerned as well. When I pray, I ask God to give me some words of encouragement and, particularly, of direction, and so I'm going to seize this text [in Mathew 13] and I'm going to, not so much exegete the complexities of the text itself, but I'm going to use it as a canvas on which to paint the current contemporary issues that are facing our society today.

This text is a parable in which Jesus talks about what the kingdom of heaven is like. And when he begins to talk about it, he compares it to a man who sowed good seed in his field. "But while men slept, his enemy came and sowed tares among the wheat, and went his way." While men slept. You need to understand that this country in many, many ways has been in a state of sleep. We've been asleep. We've been asleep spiritually. We've been asleep to the fact that we could be threatened. We've been asleep to the fact that we could be attacked at any moment. And while we were engrossed in the sleepiness and the boredom of our frivolous thinking, while we were asleep debating political issues arguing amongst Democrats and Republicans, while we were asleep pitting one race against the other, one culture against the another, while we were asleep arguing over church and state and whether you can pray at a football game or whether you can pray at a graduation ceremony—while we were asleep, America, the enemy was slipping in and creeping in and strategically planting tares amongst the wheat.

While we were asleep, busy digging through the trash can of our leaders. While we were asleep, turning our government into the Jerry Springer Show, becoming voyeurs of each other's private and sexual lives. While we were asleep, spending millions of dollars on Hollywood entertainment so we could make war games and play video games of war games, and spending millions of dollars in technology to simulate war so that we could go to movies and watch people play war. While we were asleep, using war as a cliché and talking about the war on crime and the war on drugs and the war on this and the war on that, because we have been so long without a real war that we have forgotten what war is. While we were asleep in the absence of war, we've become each other's voyeurs. Talk shows have taken over the country. We've become gossipers; we've become preoccupied with digging down in the trash cans of each other's lives for entertainment. We've traded in TV for "real TV," for using people in different situations for entertainment. While we were sleeping, arguing about percentages and interests and stock markets and investments and annuities, the enemy was stealthily creeping in our backdoor, building networks, setting up structures.

Do you hear what I'm saying? You must understand that this is deeper than one man. This is not just the workings of one man. It is far deeper than that. It goes far more intensely than anything Osama bin Laden would do. It is deeper than that. Yes, if it were one person you could easily take him out. But while we were sleeping in this country, the enemy was busy setting up networks all across this country and around the world, which has put us in a dilemma where this war will not be like any other war that we have ever had to fight. In times past, we were fighting against a country in a particular geographical location. But this enemy has sowed his tares everywhere. And when the president talks about it being a "new war," it will be a new war because the enemy is literally everywhere and our leaders are trying to trace all of his sites and all of his locations.

While we were asleep. Do you hear me? The enemy has come and planted tares amongst the wheat! I hope you hear me today, 'cause I didn't come to play patty cake with you this morning. I came to sound an alarm in Zion. And I came to serve notice on you. Yes, America has been asleep, but she's awake now. She's awake right now. Do you hear what I said? She is alive and awake right now.

Now, imagine with me. They have shut off all the boroughs around Manhattan. Completely closed down. Everything is in a state of emergency. All the police are focused on the remains and the rubble of the buildings. The firefighters who haven't been killed in it are fighting for it. Volunteers are all centered around what was the World Trade Center and yet, there were no reports for days of any lootings, of any robberies. America is awake. That's not natural. That's not normal. Nobody's bothering anything or taking anything.

Imagine with me. The president has gone to Congress and he asked for $20 billion. They gave him $40 billion. No arguments, no fighting, no political junk, and no arguing between Democrats and Republicans. Imagine with me. Who would have thought, after the bitter fight that existed for the presidency, that Al Gore and George [W.] Bush would be sitting up in church together with Bill Clinton singing songs and praying prayers. America is awake. We may have been asleep, baby, but we're not asleep now. America is wide awake.

According to the most recent polls, there is no difference between how African Americans feel and how Caucasian Americans feel about this. There is no difference in how Hispanics feel about this. The polls are coming in conclusively that all Americans are on the same page about this. So if the devil thought that while we were sleeping that we wouldn't wake up, I came to serve notice on him!

Now, let's put this into perspective. The enemy has sowed tares. When you sow tares, you sow them strategically, and there's been a strategy released. When Colin Powell begins to talk about launching a campaign, he's talking about a rigorous campaign, because the enemy has stealthily crept in and planted various things in various places in an attempt to overthrow what God would have us to have. That is freedom. Not only freedom for America, but for all of the free countries of the world is being jeopardized. The prime ministers and presidents from all over the world are calling in their support. You need to pray, right there, that all the communities, the global community, would get on the same page with us. Because the president has said that America (and I'm glad that we've lost enough arrogance to admit we need some help), America cannot win this war by herself. So we're going to need favor. (Somebody needs to send Osama bin Laden my tape, "Favor Ain't Fair.") We need favor, because we do not intend to fight fair. I said, We don't intend to fight fair.

And you must understand, my brothers and sisters, this is not about retaliation, though there are many people that are using that word *retaliation*. We don't have the luxury of retaliation. We don't have the luxury of arguing about vengeance and revenge and the theology that centers around whether we should seek revenge. This isn't about seeking revenge; this is about self-defense. It's about self-defense, because they are coming and they are coming back again. We have a short time to turn this around. And I don't mean to alarm you, but I do mean to wake you up out of your sleep. We cannot say to our young people, If you stay at home, we can spare your life. If we don't send troops in there to fight, there won't be a home for young people to stay at. A friend of mine called me and he said that walking around the streets of New York, he thought he was in Beirut. If we don't fight, you could look outside your back door tomorrow and swear *you* were in Beirut. Bullets zinging around your windows, blowing up our grandparents in their beds, destroying high-rise homes for senior citizens. Everything that we have has been threatened.

I was interviewed on CNN the other morning. Right in the middle of the interview, they stopped me and said, "Would you just pray?" On CNN. I didn't say TBN, I said CNN. "Pray for the nation." And I found myself praying for the nation on CNN. Nobody is arguing about prayer in the schools. Nobody's talking about the separation of church and state. Nobody's saying, "That prayer offended me." Nobody's offended now. Everybody wants some prayer up in here. I have been telling you for a long time that it was the vision of this church for blacks and whites and browns to come together in one place and worship God. I have been beating the pulpit telling you that it has never been God's will for there to be such things as white churches and black churches and Hispanic churches. It's rubbish, it's ridiculous. When Osama bin Laden, or whoever it was behind this treacherous act, sent those planes toward the World Trade Center, he didn't send them after black folks, he didn't send them after white folks, he didn't send them after Hispanics or Jews. He sent them after America. America. Somewhere in the Red, White, and Blue, there is you.

Now admittedly, this country has had its share of problems and it's had its share of challenges and it hasn't been right about everything, and historically we've bickered like children in the sandboxes, arguing about the issues of life. But, we bickered because there was a sandbox. Now they're about to blow up the sandbox. We've got to stop arguing about what's going on in the box, and fight for the box. Because if we don't fight for the box, they're going to come in from the outside and blow up the box, and it won't just be black folks or white folks or brown folks. It's going to be American folks.

I was in a foreign country just a couple of years ago, and they were treating me kind of funny and I couldn't figure out why. I'd never been looked at quite like that. I could tell it wasn't a friendly look; it was a little hostile look, but it was a different look than what I was accustomed to. I couldn't understand it. Some Africans were in the same country, and [the natives] treated them very nicely. So I ruled out my first thought; being raised in this country, I thought it was a color issue. But when they treated the Africans, who happened to be darker than me, better than me, suddenly, I realized it wasn't color. I was all the way back home before I realized they hated me for being American. I'm used to being hated for being black. I've kinda gotten used to that. But now when I'm out of the country, I'm hated for being American. Something about being hated for being American suddenly drove home the fact that, regardless of the color of my skin, I am very much American.

These people that are coming against us are coming against our country, not our color. They're coming against our country, not our politics. They're coming against out country, not our lifestyle, and we had better come together, "one nation, under God, indivisible, with liberty and justice for all." You don't hear what I'm saying to you. I want to sound the alarm this morning. I want to blow the trumpet in your ears. It's high time for you to wake out of your sleep. And yes, we're hurt. And yes, we're weeping. And yes, we're angry. And don't tell me that just because I'm a Christian I shouldn't be angry. Jesus was angry and cleared the temple. The Bible said, "Be angry and sin not." Sometimes you're going to need anger. You're going to need fire to drive you, but you don't want to be reckless with the anger. This is a significant point.

You must understand that Osama bin Laden and all of his activities do not represent the Muslim theology. And so you've got to be careful because there are millions of Arab Americans who love this country like we do. So you can't start harassing people because they look different or because they worship differently. They are still Americans. Do you hear what I'm saying? I am a Christian. I'm unashamedly a Christian. And I'm proud to be a Christian. And I don't agree with the theology of the Muslims. But, I do defend their right to believe what they believe. I defend their right to worship the way they want to worship. And, I defend my right to disagree with how they worship. But that is what America is all about—the freedom to worship. Don't allow people to push you into going out at random and picking people who look like Osama bin Laden and attacking them, because if anybody ought to understand racial profiling—! Come on, come on.

It's time for you to stand up. So we've got to be angry, but we can't be reckless. We can't be sinful and we can't be disrespectful. What we need is a cold, calculated, God-given strategy.

So, there's a debate going on. From whence cometh these tares? From whence did they come? What happened? We just woke up and all of a sudden our buildings are blowing up. And everybody is trying to find out, why did this happen? So everybody's looking at our foreign policy. They're looking at our government's posture. They're looking at how things were done. The preachers are all standing up. And all of them are trying to say, Why did this happen? We're trying to explain God. God doesn't need an explanation. We don't need to try to explain the mind of God; we need to teach people the mercy of God. Who can know the mind of God? God said, "My thoughts are above your thoughts, my ways above your ways." We don't need to explain God. And so, people are trying to say, "Well God did it." Not mine! Not mine! Maybe yours, not mine. The God that I've been worshiping all of these years is not a God that would send a 747 into the World Trade Center and kill at random innocent, praying, godly people—not my God. Not the one I lift my hands to and worship. No, I do not believe it! And you cannot make me believe it. The Bible said clearly, "An enemy has done this." Don't you put that on God! Don't you get deep and spiritual and condescending and self-righteous and act like God is judging America. If God has been merciful to the world, I believe that that same God would be merciful to America. This is not the workings of God; this is the workings of an enemy. The Bible said, "An enemy has done this." Don't let anybody tell you this is God. And you don't even have to fight over it. Just stand on the fact that our God is a just God. He's a holy God. He's a loving God. He's a merciful God.

God knows how to capitalize on what the enemy did. For the Bible said, "For all things work together for the good of them who love the Lord." Maybe the devil did do it, but God's going to take that which the devil meant for evil and make it turn out for good because America is gathering together. We're coming together. We're praying together. We're worshiping together. We're uniting our forces together, and I want to serve notice on the devil: *You ain't seen nothing yet.* Clap your hands like you understand what I'm saying.

There must be a separation in our understanding between government and church. We must understand that the Bible said that the powers that be (talking about the government) are ordained of God. Don't allow people to overwhelm you with "If you were really a Christian you should not be interested in revenge." First of all, it's not revenge, nor is it retaliation; it's self-defense. Second thing you need to understand is the decision to go to war is not going to come from the pulpit. It is not coming from the pulpit; it is coming from the White House. And according to the Scriptures, we are supposed to support those who are in positions of power. We cannot weigh them down this time with our religious rhetoric. We need to be on our knees praying. And if Osama bin Laden or whoever was involved behind him and with him and the countries who supported him are laughing today because they have knocked America to their knees, let me explain that when America gets on her knees, it's not because she's defeated, baby. It's because she's getting ready to fight. My war position is on my knees. I'll knock you out from my knees! I'll overcome my enemies on my knees. If I've been knocked to my knees, I'm going to fight on my knees.

Touch three people and say, "Let's get together." Black folk, white folk, red folk, brown folk, rich folk, poor folk, educated, illiterate: Let's get together. No bickering, no complaining, no murmuring, no fighting. Let's stand together. Together we stand, united we fall. Let's get together. And so my brothers and sisters, when you pray, ask God to give our president, our Commander in Chief and all of his advisors, to give them divine strategies, supernatural wisdom, agility of wit, articulation of speech. Ask God to make the president cunning. Right now we need somebody cunning. We don't need anybody cute. We don't need a mamby-pamby, soft-baked, freeze-dried president. We need somebody that's shrewd, and the public doesn't need to know everything. You can't fight this kind of enemy if your strategies are going to be all over CNN. And so God says in the parable, God says to them, he says, Don't you move quickly and try to separate the wheat from the tares, lest in the process of getting the tares, you destroy the wheat.

And the issue before us now, since these networks, these cells, are set up all over our country and other countries—[the issue] is how to get in and pull out the tares with the most minimal amount of damage to the wheat. It's not like they're all in one place. We need a shrewd God-given strategy, tip-toeing up stealthily on this enemy.

But this enemy has got to go. If we have to go get some boys from the hood, he's got to come out of here now. He's got to go. He's got to go. This is not optional. This is not optional. It wasn't my country when I got here, but it is now. My ancestors' blood is running down into the soils of this country. You're not going to run me up out of here. Nah, nah, nah. If slavery didn't run me out, if the civil rights movement didn't run me out, if being beat with a water hose didn't run me out, if the trouble you went through didn't run you out, if people came here from all walks of life and they endured hardships and overcame the Depression and withstood the second World War and stood here, then no terrorist group is going to run us out of here. Not without the fight of your life. And I believe to my soul, if we fight and if we pray, we'll win.

Let me quickly caution you that this will not be easy. Congress has approved $40 billion to fight, but the real cost will not be dollars; it will be lives. It will be body bags. It will be our sons and daughters. This is not a cliché of war. This is real war, and this is not the kind of war that President Bush can confer with other presidents about and figure out how they did it because this is a new kind of war. So the churches need to pray everywhere.

The question arises, How do we talk to our children? Some have said, Just comfort the children and tell them everything is going to be okay. That's not going to work. You cannot teach your children this Santa-Claus, ice-cream-cone mentality that we've had the luxury of enjoying while we were asleep. You have got to educate your children as to what is happening and what it means, not to terrorize them but to train them. Baby doll, if you look out there and you see a strange man drop a suitcase in a strange place, then you've got to get out of there quickly. You cannot train children if you have lulled them to sleep in a false sense of security. Not while *their* children are carrying M-16s up and down the street. America has got to grow up, and we've only got this weekend to get it done. Whether you realize it or not, our sons and daughters, black, white, and brown, have already got their papers. [The military is] already starting to move them into positions. Some of them have already left. This is real. The urgency in Colin Powell's voice is staggering.

As I talk to major news commentators across the country, news commentators who have covered some of the greatest atrocities of our age are breaking into tears. This is a critical issue. This is no joke. I have a rule when I fly on a plane that when the plane hits an air pocket and it scares me, I always look to the flight attendant, and if the flight attendant is still smiling, I go back to reading the paper. But if I turn to her and her skin looks scaly and her eyes are bucked and her skin is unusually white, I put my book up and get my prayer cloth out. And, when I look at this nation's leaders and I see their lips trembling, when I see them holding hands and praying with people who they were arguing with last week, when I see news commentators getting choked up in the middle of what would normally have been be a professional dissertation, I know it's some real trouble up in here.

The Lord said, "In the time of harvest, I will come in and I will gather the tares into bundles." So I want you to pray that God would expose the enemy. Expose him. Everywhere. Anywhere. Expose his devices. Pray that God exposes his tactics. Expose him on foreign soils. Expose him if he's got spies in our government. Expose him because they've broken our codes and they've entered into our computer systems. Expose him on technology. You've got to put your King James English up and start praying up to date. We're not fighting no two-thousand-year-old demon. This is a 2001 contemporary, twenty-first century devil who is hacking into our computer systems. We have to pray against hackers. You gotta start praying in tongues and praying in the Holy Ghost, and watch and pray and believe God. And God said, "In the time of harvest." Tell Osama bin Laden, "It's harvest time." Tell the demonic forces behind him, "It's harvest time." Tell every country that's harboring these enemies, "It's harvest time." God said,

"In the time of harvest, I will bind the tares into bundles to burn them."

See, it's not "Am I going to fight?" It's not "Is the country going to fight?" The only thing that the devil needs to know is that God is going to fight. And if God be for us, *who?* Shake somebody's hand and tell them, "The Lord is on my side." Don't you turn on me because the Lord is on my side! And when it's all said and done—we're going to win!

I'm going to hasten to a close, but I want to tell you quickly, all that stuff you've been singing about and all the things you've been praying about and all the things we've been rehearsing, have been getting us ready. And while America has been asleep, the church has been preparing for spiritual warfare for a long time. See, we got to fight like Moses fought. The Bible said that Moses got up on the mountain and lifted up his hands, and while he lifted up his hands, Joshua fought in the valley. And the church has got to assume the position of Moses and lift up holy hands before God and begin to call upon the name of the Lord. Let Colin Powell be the Joshua that goes down in the valley and begins to fight. But let the preachers and the leaders of the religious institutions lift up holy hands and call on the name of our God. And the God who hears in secret will reward you openly. And, no weapon—no weapon!—formed against you shall prosper, and every tongue that rises against you, God will condemn.

Reconciliation: Beyond Retaliation

Gardner C. Taylor

SEPTEMBER 18, 2001

O ne comes to this hour with strange, surging emotions. All of us have had indelibly impressed upon our memories where we were and how the intelligence first reached us of this tragedy, which has changed America forever. I had flown from Chicago on a Monday evening and was called by my friend Vernon Jordan at ten o'clock in the morning and told to turn on the television and look and see. And after that viewing I am convinced that we have entered now a new era of our lives.

When I grew up years ago, we were taught that our country was protected by two oceans and that we were invulnerable to attack. Last Tuesday changed all of that. And for the lives of all of you, for the lifespan of all of you, things will be different than what they were last Monday night and early last Tuesday. Our first response, I suppose, is almost inevitable. It is of shock, horror, and the desire for retaliation. I am not a full disciple of nonviolence. I used to argue with Dr. King about this. I believe the Civil War should have been fought. I believe that the world had an obligation to put down the plague of Adolf Hitler. And for all of us it would be too much to ask of human beings not to want some kind of retaliation, some kind of thwarting of this horror, of this monstrous thing that has happened within our country. So we pass through that period, but Lord help us if we stay there!

talked with a man yesterday afternoon and he said what we need to do is to bomb all of them. "Wipe them out. Send them all,"—he said this not in a reverential way, but in a pejorative way—"Bomb them all to Allah." I was totally shocked, speechless—until he told me also that he was member of Alcoholics Anonymous and he had missed last Friday's session! But I'm afraid, gravely so, that his sentiments of retaliation, which likely could be explained by time spent with bottled spirits, stand perched on the lips of so many who have not been near alcohol, but are instead inebriated by a spirit that we can not allow to inhabit us. We must move beyond it, we must.

Beyond retaliation we must focus upon something else. And I think that something was best expressed in this morning's *New York Times* Letters to the Editor. The first letter came from Rita Lasar who said this: "My brother Abe Zelmanowitz was on the twenty-seventh floor of the World Trade Center when the first plane hit. Although he could have gotten out of the building he chose instead to stay with his friend, a quadriplegic who could not get out. President Bush mentioned his heroism in his speech at the National Cathedral on Friday. It is in my brother's name and mine that I pray that we, this country that has been so deeply hurt, not do something that will unleash forces we will not have the power to call back."

And those of us who have known the awful experience of someone going out and never coming back—suddenly struck down—have some sense of how much it took of charity and of a sense of our common humanity for that woman to write this letter. This is not a time for brash statements and for intemperate comments, some of which have been made by some of our religious leaders, who claim a relationship to God which their statements contradicted. And this is not a time for any ten-gallon-hat riding-into-the-sunset idea of frontier justice. If America now descends to the level of evil which has been inflicted upon it, then we are lost. And I could understand the sentiments of the people at our highest levels of government who feel not only the horror and anger we all feel, but who also have one eye turned toward their constituency. Our leadership must rise above the pedestrian and barbaric. This is not a time for "dead or alive" talk. This is a time for the most mature consideration of American justice to have their place.

Beyond retaliation we must think of reconciliation. And there is a passage in the second book of Chronicles which I think ought to characterize and motivate and direct and guide us all. This Scripture depicts a time of pride. Solomon is dedicating the temple in all of its glory. The people are proud, prosperous, and engaged in revelry. But heaven has a word for them during this period. God says in the fourteenth verse of the seventh chapter of 2 Chronicles, "If my people, which are called by my name, shall humble themselves, and pray, and seek my face, and turn from their wicked ways; then will I hear from heaven, and will forgive their sin, and will heal their land" (KJV). Now in our most sober and deepest sense, these are the spirits we must seek—a spirit of humbleness and prayer, a spirit of seeking God and falling away from our own wickedness, our own trespasses.

We can be instructed theologically at this point by the Greeks. You are familiar with the Greek tragedies. They are all about heroes and heroines caught in the toils of circumstances that they cannot control. They see the way out, but the more they risk, the more trapped and helpless they are. Why? Because for the Greeks, the ultimate transgression is to defy or assault the preeminence of their gods. Much of our Western civilization has taken its cue directly from the Greeks, and so there is no hope that our civilization will not go the way of the Greeks unless we learn how to hold power and humility in balance. God is the ultimate power source, and if we are wise, we kneel humbly before him, ever seeking his guidance in instances where power is to be utilized.

As William A. Jones and I talked last night as he said to me, "There is 'conscienceless power.' And there is 'powerless conscience.'" Where power is not regulated by conscience, it becomes arrogance and brutality. Where conscience is not supported by power, it becomes futility. Thus, our primary responsibility now in this country is to humble ourselves, to recognize that we have not been perfect in the world, nor have we been the worst. We have seen glorious acts of heroism and faithfulness and perseverance on the part of the people at World Trade Center and all through this country, there is a feeling of mutuality.

We hope that the Lord will grant that, not just for the moment but beyond, so that we may deal, if we humanly can, with the question of whether this country can bring together its power and humility. We have to ask ourselves, Why are we hated so around the world? Now, in one sense power inevitably invites resentment. But if we are going to be a nation under God, then by the grace of God, our power and our humility and our sense of being a part of the human family must come together. If our power is unaccompanied by humility, we're lost to the kingdom of God. And on the other side, if our humility is unaccompanied by power, we're lost in this kind of world. Our only hope is that the power we have will be brought together with humility and restraint.

And people on the margins of this society—minority people—will be a part of helping this happen. W. E. B Du Bois said back in the early part of the last century that there is "a two-ness" in being black in America, being *in* it and yet not quite *of* it, reaping its benefits yet feeling some of its stings of injustice. Minority people are now peculiarly and, I believe, providentially endowed by God to speak to the nation and say that pride brings ruin and that this country must look to reconciliation.

Retaliation, very well, but reconciliation must be our ultimate aim unless we want to risk utter ruin. We will never bomb hatred out of the world. Hatred produces hatred. The history of the world is replete with that, and somehow, we have not learned the lesson. We've fought war after war after war. First, World War I to save the world for democracy. Then, the next one to rid the world of the evil of narcissism, and on and on. When will someone step forward and say, "Beyond retaliation to reconciliation"?

So in our acts of kindness and in our spirit of patriotism, let us most serve our country by pointing out what the country needs to do. In an address at the Anti-Imperialism Conference in 1899 in Chicago, Paul Scherer, quoting John Crittendon, said, "My country right or wrong. When right, to be kept right. When wrong, to help set it right. That is the only mission that's worthy of citizenship."

And so my friends, hurt, bruised, and with fear, I get on an airplane in a day or two. We must go forward, but let us go forward in faith and in faithfulness. Let us forge ahead, confident that we are not in this alone. Someone has said, that the Prophet Mohammed, traveling between Mecca and Medina, was with another friend who remarked how difficult the journey had been for the two of them. Mohammed responded to his friend, "We are not two, we are three." And our Lord said to us, "Lo, I am with you always." So, let us go forth in faith and in faithfulness and forge ahead, and leave the rest to God.

That's Enough

Walter S. Thomas

SEPTEMBER 16, 2001

Then Jesus asked them, "When I sent you without purse, bag or sandals, did you lack anything?" "Nothing," they answered. He said to them, "But now if you have a purse, take it, and also a bag; and if you don't have a sword, sell your cloak and buy one. It is written: 'And he was numbered with the transgressors'; and I tell you that this must be fulfilled in me. Yes, what is written about me is reaching its fulfillment." The disciples said, "See, Lord, here are two swords." "That is enough," he replied. —Luke 22:35-38, NIV

T hey said, "Look, Master, two swords!" But he said, "Enough of that! No more sword talk!"

This week our nation was shocked and riveted to the core as we watched with horror what the news media has termed "The Attack on America." In a matter of minutes, the security we enjoy was snatched from us as we saw the symbols of the economy and the military struck by commercial jets hijacked and turned into weapons of mass destruction. This day will never be forgotten. This day will be etched in our minds. This day shall live in infamy. Airlines have not resumed their full schedules, the FBI and CIA are working without relief. Public servants who work with disasters have reordered their lives, hopefully to bring closure to this mega-catastrophe. We have watched from every angle the scene of the 767 jets plowing into the

World Trade Center. The icons of the American economy are now history. The invincible national military might has been penetrated. The president has been forced to turn from the rebuilding of America to a retaliatory strike. At Pearl Harbor we knew the enemy, we knew his address, but today we do not know the enemy, we do not have his address. This is the terror of terrorism. The enemy can be beside you working and working with you. He or she can be a dinner guest, a business associate, and a personal friend.

Terrorism is real and comes in all forms. The FBI agent who traded secrets with the Russians, the computer hackers who shut down our networks and destroy national data, the business that pirates secrets and develops the plans of another. We remember the Munich Massacre at the 1972 Olympics when the international games were interrupted by terrorists. Many died as Black September launched its attack. Since 1993, three doctors, two clinic employees, a clinic escort, and a security guard have been murdered; sixteen attempted murders have also occurred since 1991—all of this done in the name of life, as abortion foes have sought to make their position known. Their cause may be just but their tactics terrorize. Oklahoma felt the effects of domestic terrorism as the Federal Building was destroyed, not by Arabs but by Americans. Columbine saw our nation shocked with disbelief as school-aged boys went on the rampage. Ireland has seen the awful affects of terrorism. Israel and Palestine live under the threat every day. They have lived so long on the edge of the cliff that they have just put down roots and learned to survive.

There are so many terrorist groups, more than we can number. Yet not all terrorists are on the government watch list. Many do not carry that official designation. There are terrorists in our neighborhoods selling drugs and destroying communities. There are terrorists on our jobs who intimidate people and manipulate workers. There are terrorists in our families. They have robbed us of our joy and security with outbreaks of violence, both physical and emotional. To be honest, even in the body of Christ, there are those who qualify. There are persons in the church who will smile in your face and then stab you in your back. We need to ask each other the question, "Are you a terrorist?" All over the world, terrorism is waving its flag and rattling its saber.

Simply put, terrorism is about ideas and approaches. It is about what people will do to get their way. It is the lengths that persons will go to force the hand of their enemy. I have come to understand that terrorism, regardless of who perpetrates it, runs contrary to the teachings of our faith. Albert Camus, the French existentialist, wrote a book entitled *The Rebel,* and in it he states that the rebel is not free until the oppressor has become his brother. Freedom means that blacks and whites must see each other as brothers and sisters. Each and every race must be able to use the term *brother* and create a sense of brotherhood and sisterhood. We are living with terror and hatred, Siamese twins who walk and talk together.

Some have asked, "Where was God in all of this? How could God allow this?" My friend Bishop Jakes was asked if he thought that God is taking humanity on, that human beings and God are at war. Bishop Jakes replied, "Oh no, not in the least. Because if this were a war between God and man, it'd be over already." This is a war between human being and human being, and yet persons are asking, "Where's God? Where's God in all of this? Where is God in what happened in New York? Where's God in what happened in Washington?" God is right where God has always been. He is still on the throne of power.

On Tuesday, God showed us that there are some things God will allow. Yet God also taught us on Tuesday that there are some things God will not allow. Where was God? There was a steel core that ran through the middle of the World Trade Center; the heat from the flames was so great that it melted the steel core that ultimately caused the collapse of the building. The exploding jet fuel was too great for the building to withstand. Hundreds of thousands of tons of steel and concrete came crashing down to the ground. Somebody said, "Where was God?" I'll tell you where God was. God kept the building standing longer than anyone anticipated, longer than anybody believed it could stand. Over 50,000 persons are in that area every day, but God led many of them to safety. God sent angels to aid the evacuation. Don't tell me God wasn't there!

Where was God? It is reported that the downed plane [near Pittsburgh, Pennsylvania,] was headed for the White House or the Capitol, the symbols of the democracy we have cherished. If the plane had hit the White House, it would have gone up like a tinderbox; it is not a superstructure. It is predominantly a wood building. If the plane had hit the Capitol

Building, the entire legislative branch of the United States government would have been wiped out in one flash second! Our government system would have faced a crisis the likes of which has never been seen. But God did not allow that to take place and have our lives totally decimated. Where was God? Where was God?

A friend called me to tell me that his nephew worked in the World Trade Center. Because he wanted to rise in the company, the nephew had been extremely punctual about his job. He knew this was the way to progress up the corporate ladder. That morning he overslept—and his life was spared. A lady came to me Wednesday to share her report. Her daughter was scheduled to be a flight attendant on [American] Flight 77. When she went to the airport, ready to handle her assignment, she was told that she was needed to take a flight to Chicago. The plane she was originally scheduled to work flew into the Pentagon while she flew to Chicago. Tell me God's not there!

Where's God? Terrorists often operate in cells. We do not know how many cells there are in America, but what we do know is that God kept his hand on us and said, That's enough, that is all that will happen this day. Where's God? God is on God's throne, being God.

The politicians have promised the president support. The American people feel violated and want an appropriate response. Flags are waving and the military is mobilizing and preparing a response. We are going to enter a siege mentality. We're ready to take up the gauntlet. On the night that Michael Dukakis lost his bid for the presidency of the United States, the talking heads were on television trying to give a rationale for Dukakis's defeat and Bush's victory. Some said that he could not overcome the Willie Horton scandal. Some said that he just didn't look presidential; others added that he was too liberal. But then one of the pundits stood up with a rationale that defined the American ethos. He said that Dukakis lost because when asked the question in the debate about how he would respond if he wife were assaulted, attacked, and what he would do, his answer was weak. He would make sure she got counseling and treatment and he would give her support. That was the answer that cost him the election. He lost because in the words of the guest, he did not understand America. Americans want revenge!

And I submit to you today, my brothers and sisters, though we may talk about revenge and retaliation, there is something else we must raise as a topic of deep concern. We must talk about repentance. Do not think I'm saying that we do not need to retaliate. There are persons who say, "We don't believe in violence, we don't believe that you should strike back." But understand this truth. The reason one can be a pacifist is because somebody else defends your freedom. The reason you can say "I will not fight" is because somebody else will fight for the rights we enjoy. There will be many who will say, "I don't believe we ought to strike back, we ought to do this..." You must understand that in this life, we must stand up against oppression and aggression. You must, I must, we must.

Am I advocating violence? Am I saying that this is the appropriate response? I am telling you what is going to happen. I'm telling you that you are going to hear bombs blasting. I'm telling you that you are going to see missiles flying. I'm telling you that you are going to see troops mobilized. I'm telling you, loved ones are getting on boats and planes and traveling to the Middle East. I'm telling you that this is going to happen. But God sent me in this house to declare that when we talk about retaliation we must also talk about repentance. It is not unpatriotic to discuss our response need and our need to repent. We cannot just strike without also searching our hearts.

Life moves by cause and effect. Whenever we examine a situation, we must look at the forces that brought it into being. We must understand both internal and external causations. We must look at the motivating forces that surround a situation. Now the effect is the product, the result that comes from the situation. There was a cause and there are effects. The incident is the crash; the cause is terrorism and hatred. The result, the effect, is loss of life and a need to strike back with force. Now listen, retaliation is a response to an effect. Five thousand are missing, presumed dead. Yesterday they showed for the first time the footage of what really happened. America has been violated! Our land's been hit, our lifestyle's been attacked. And the carnage! There are children who will have no parents, boys and girls who will be orphaned. There are just last words on an answering machine saying "I love you." With that much rage building in the hearts of America, there will be a response.

We are looking with suspicion at every Arab and everyone from the Middle East. The *angst* of the moment has caused us to lose perspective. If the bombers had been African Americans, we would be suspect. If they had been Chinese, then all Chinese would be suspect. If they had been Irish, then we would feel that way toward [the Irish]. The desire to retaliate has made us lose sight of our sensibilities.

One cannot be violated at that level and not act. To avoid action is to open the door for it to happen again. My parents had to discipline me when I violated the policies of home, because not to would undermine not only their authority but the continuation of the family. Whether they wanted to or not, they had to respond. I had to know that they knew the significance of my infraction.

Yet, I submit to you that we need more than revenge; we need repentance. Revenge and retaliation deal with the effects of the violence. We want revenge because we feel violated. Repentance, however, deals with the cause of the action. The death makes us want to retaliate, but the pain makes us need to repent.

In the midst of our national mourning, let us not forget our complicity. Anyone who speaks in such a manner is called unpatriotic, but the Master says, "The truth will set us free," and freedom is the real issue. We must be able to separate the reason for the deed from the effects of the deed. There is no word to justify the death of so many. There is no language that gives credence and support for so heinous a deed. The effects are devastating. But our hands are not clean. We took prayer out of schools. We made God a second-class deity in the land he founded. We made profits more important than prayer. We pushed God to the back burner. Now we sing the songs of our nation, but we need to sing the hymns of our faith. Violence begets violence. It is time for us to call the world, the nation, our city, our families, and ourselves to repentance. It is time to seek God's face and to declare that God alone is worthy to be praised. George W. Bush can plan a response, but the church of the living Lord must call for repentance.

There is an interesting story in the Gospels about one of the final encounters the Master had with his disciples. Jesus is offering the world a new way of living and a new way of relating. He has healed, delivered, and blessed, and as such he created a new community. His advance guard, the twelve disciples, will be the leaders of the new community. The battle lines have been drawn and the Master is in the center. What will be his stance when the fighting starts? Will he lead his troops into battle? Will he make himself known and call for all-out war? What will be his approach?

The Bible reports that the Master met with the Twelve and discussed the future. As they neared the end of their gathering, the Master makes a major speech. They have been out there struggling to begin his kingdom, and the battle has not been easy, but he asks them a question. "What did you lack?" The answer, "Nothing." That is crucial. They had everything they needed to do the work they were assigned. Even though they faced persons who hated them and despised their position, they had all they needed for the situation. The Master knew he would die, but he wanted them to realize that their strength was different from that of their adversaries.

When they went forward in his name, they had everything they needed. This is a powerful truth. They were fully equipped, equipped by God with his Word. Most of us are looking for something else to add to our arsenal so as to be ready to take on the forces of life. The revenge syndrome makes us want to give into the dark side and become the very force we abhor. We want to add violence to our array of weapons. When someone hurts us, abuses us, disappoints us, and seeks to destroy us, our natural inclination is to strike back. Yet the Master says, You were always equipped for what they did to you. They have not won nor will they win. They will be defeated. God works with what he gives us to accomplish what must be done. That is what empowerment is all about. We may be attacked but the attack does not have to have the effect of making us look elsewhere for support.

The psalmist declared it correctly: "My help comes from the Lord, the maker of heaven and earth." Regardless of what happens to us, our help comes from the Lord. This is the response that God wants us to have when we are confronted with the terror that strikes our lives. Do not forget that the Lord is with you. He was with those who went down in flames, those who died in the collapse of the buildings. He is always there. I know that we want to retaliate, but the method must be correct.

That night when the mob came after Jesus, Peter pulled a sword and attacked. Jesus stopped him and said, "He who lives by the sword shall die by the sword." Violence changes the persons who participate in it. From street gangs to international terrorists, such actions change the participants. When the men and women returned from the Vietnam War, the Korean conflict, and World War II, they reported that they were changed by their role in the war. Violence makes us rethink our own moral fabric and our own moral code. This is why violent thinking must be killed in our minds. When Martin King died, we rioted. In Watts, Newark, and around the country, riots broke out. When Rodney King was beaten and the perpetrators were released, we rioted. We fight but that thought must be held captive by the truth that God will never fail us. We must kill the violent thought.

Am I saying that we do nothing? No, I am saying that before we do anything, we need to repent. We need to return to the Lord and ask forgiveness for our sins. We must clean our hands and ask God to forgive us of our mistakes and shortcomings. We must work for a better world; we must be a better people. This is the lesson from the incident. The deaths cannot be in vain. Yes, the perpetrators must be brought to justice, but we must become a better people as a result of this.

I love this country. I know there are those who do not, who say, "I don't love America." The people who hate us do not know the "US" I know. Many persons around this world see America as the beast because we have allowed too many of the wrong people to talk for us and to present our case. A columnist some years ago, James Kilpatrick, spoke it best, "America does not have friends; it has interests." America does not have friends, just interests. Why do we worry so much about the Persian Gulf? Is it the people or the oil? The people of God must say we don't abide by that philosophy anymore. When you have an opportunity to speak, ask God to give you a word. These are tough times and righteous people must make righteous declarations. If the world is to know that America is God-fearing, God-loving, and people-loving, then military might is not going to teach it. Those of us who have been transformed by God must do the work.

I close by saying, when you get home, grab your family and say, It's time for us to pray a repentance prayer because we've not been what we should have been, and ask God to bless America. We must begin to pray from our hearts and pour out our souls unto the Lord. It is not about asking God to bless America to be rich, or to bless America to be free from trouble. It is time to pray, "God, we're not all we should be. We want you to bless our country, restore our spirit, give us the right minds. Help us to learn to love everybody; help us to learn to treat our neighbor right." It's praying time. It's repentance time.

God showed us Tuesday that, no matter how big and powerful we are, we need him. While the nation, the national leaders, plan the response, let us come to realize through this that we need God at a deeper level. Don't come to church just because this is the Sunday after the bombing. Don't say, "Well, maybe I need to get back into church." You needed to get back before you said maybe.

What we saw Tuesday is the epitome, the personification of the idea that "It's got to be my way." We saw it carried to its ultimate conclusion without care or concern for collateral damage. Don't let that spirit live in you at any level. Kill that spirit! That's what blew up the World Trade Center. "I'm gonna do what I got to do, I just don't care who doesn't like it." No! Kill that spirit! That's what wiped out part of the Pentagon. "I mean, I just got to be me, this is just the way I am." No! That cost more than 260 people in the air their lives. "Well, I just don't care who doesn't like it." No! Don't talk like that. That cost more than three hundred fire-fighters and police officers their opportunity to go back home. Kill it in you so that it doesn't have a place to feel at home.

Jesus said, "That's enough sword talk." America's gonna respond, but you and I have a Pentecost date. You and I will not have a say on what will be the military response. But what you and I can be in charge of is the effort to make this world, and the kingdoms of this world, become the kingdoms of our God.

When the disciples said they had swords, Jesus said, "No more talk about swords." It is time to talk about the kingdom and now is kingdom time. God has made us aware that we need his hand and his guidance. We need the power of the Lord. You see the times are tough and the way of life is stranger. There is only one who can help us in these dark days. It is war, but we have the God of life on our side. This is the time to turn to him and seek his face. He is Jehovah Jireh. He is the God who provides. Jesus went to that cross without a weapon in hand, but his faith and trust in God was rewarded on Easter Sunday morning.

As we go forward, let us end the talk of swords and start the talk about salvation. It is saving time. If ever we needed the Lord we need him now. I have come to declare: He is here and ready to receive us. We have been hurt, but he is the comforter. Let him hold you until the hurts are healed.

Come, ye disconsolate, where'er ye languish.
Come to the mercy seat, fervently kneel;
Here bring your wounded hearts, here tell your anguish:
Earth has no sorrow that heav'n cannot heal.

Amen.

Prophesy
in Times
Like These

What's Going On?

Charles E. Booth

September 16, 2001

And they glorified God ..., saying, "We have seen strange things."
—Luke 5:26, NRSV

Many years ago, on the seventh day of December 1941, when Pearl Harbor was attacked by the Japanese, then President Franklin Delano Roosevelt echoed the phrase that has very much been on the lips of men and women since that fateful day. He declared that "this day will live in infamy." I think today that I can say without fear of contradiction that all of us would agree that such a phrase is applicable to what occurred on Tuesday, September 11. Regardless of how old or young we might be, all of us will remember where we were and what we were doing when those first images of jets hitting the Twin Towers of the World Trade Center and demolishing structures that we thought were literally indestructible.

We have seen things this week that we never dreamed of seeing. And indeed, they are defined and registered in our minds as strange things. Who would have thought that terrorists would have taken commercial jets, representing two of the strongest airlines in American history—American Airlines and United—and plowed those tremendous jets into the Twin Towers of the World Trade Center? The persons who are responsible for this heinous crime are obviously very intelligent people. It is one of the most well or-chestrated and choreographed crimes ever known to humankind. We got up today in what is a cloak of sadness, and whether we want to admit it or not, there is a darkness that holds over the moral and spiritual landscape, not only of our country, but of our world. There are many people who are declaring, How could such a thing happen in what we have called the greatest experiment in democracy that the world has ever known? We have seen strange things this week.

Little children are wondering now what kind of world we truly live in. This is the kind of thing that we see on television. This is the stuff of which science fiction is made. These are the kinds of things that our children have been looking at in the movies for years. And now we see that what we thought was simply in the movies is now real life. People are dead in New York, people are dead in Washington, D.C. There are not many of us talking about those who perished in the airline crash outside of Pittsburgh, in what many believe, and I number among those, was a diverted effort away from our nation's capital. We have seen strange things this week.

In one context, they are strange, but to those of us who are a part of the church, those of us who are a part of the community of faith, these things are not strange at all. These are things that have been prophesied. The problem is that many of us don't believe in prophecy. Or perhaps I should really restate that. Many of us believe in prophecies of a particular ilk and kind. We believe in these modern-day soothsayers who come among us to prophesy that money cometh. And many of us will sit in congregations if we can find somebody who will tell us that our purses will be fattened and that our material lives and tangible assets will be increased. I don't know where these people are today. They can prophesy that your blessing in ma-terial wealth is coming; they can prophesy that God has a man for you somewhere down the road; they can prophesy that there is a woman some-where waiting just around the bend. But not one of them could prophesy the terror that fell out of the sky in New York, the horror that fell out of the sky in Washington, D.C., and the agonizing reality that took people to their death outside of Pittsburgh, Pennsylvania.

In the fifth chapter of Luke, the Spirit of God has come mightily upon his Son, and Luke records that he is primed and ready to heal. Enormous numbers of people are brought to Jesus as he ministers in a home somewhere in Capernaum. (Many believe it is Peter's home.) And the number of those to be healed is so great that the building in which they gather is overflowing, so much so that people are literally out of the door and into the street. Somewhere in the crowd there is a paralytic who has been brought to this site of healing by his friends. They are not able to come through any one of the doors. They are not able to go through any one of the windows. They decide that they will go up on the roof, peel back its thatched makeup, and lower their paralytic friend in the midst of the crowd, and literally sit him at the Master's feet. And their thinking is wise because once the eyes of the Master fall upon this paralytic man, he immediately begins the grand adventure of healing. Be quick to notice that he does not lay his hands immediately upon the paralytic's limbs to heal him, but he first begins by forgiving the man of his sins. Jesus understands that there cannot be physical healing until there is first internal and spiritual healing.

What a word for all of us today who believe in the power of God. Sometimes we wonder why God does not do anything in our physical and tangible world. It is because we have not yet let God do what God must do in our spiritual world in order to make healing complete. God never does anything incomplete. The man's sins are forgiven, the man's paralytic condition is transformed, it's converted, it's healed. And the Pharisees and teachers who have a legitimate right to be there because deuteronomic law says that whenever a new rabbi or teacher appears on the scene that person must be looked at to make sure that what he is doing falls within Mosaic parameters. And they look at Jesus and hear him forgive sins. They immediately call him one who blasphemes. But their criticism is put on hold when the man is healed. And when the man picks up his couch and walks out of the building, they look at one another, scratch their heads, and declare, "We have seen strange things this day."

The World Trade Center no longer exists today; the Pentagon has a wing totally destroyed. And I don't know about you but I praise God for life. I think one week ago on Saturday I flew out of La Guardia, saw the Twin Towers, saw the Empire State Building, saw the Chrysler Building, saw Shea Stadium, and saw Arthur Ashe Stadium, where Venus and Serena

Williams made history. I had not an inkling at all that in a few short days the Twin Towers that represent our economic prosperity would disintegrate literally in what these physicists call implosion. Whoever masterminded the terrorist attacks, particularly on the World Trade Center, had an understanding of physics. They were not dummies. Don't you think for one minute that whoever did it was stupid. No, No. They were highly intelligent men. And one of these days you're gonna wake up and hear me: The devil creates chaos and confusion, but he is not chaotic nor is he confused. He knows exactly what he is doing and how he intends to do it.

Somehow or another we've got to discover and determine what God is saying to us. I debated whether or not I would say this but I may as well say it now. It is not so much what I say, but it's what Dr. Cornell West, professor of philosophy and religion at Harvard University, said on the radio the other day. He said that maybe for the first time the world understands what it means to be a nigger in America. I believe him, but I didn't say it. For those of us who are African American, we know what it is to be hit by jumbo jets while we are minding our own business. Now the nation must understand how Emmett Till must have felt. We now understand how those four little black girls felt in the Sixteenth Street Baptist Church in Birmingham, Alabama, in August of 1963. Now we know what Martin King felt when out of nowhere comes an element of destruction and turns our world upside down.

What's going on? Does the world now belong to Satan? Is the world now in the hands of terrorists? Has God gone on holiday and left us to our own demonic destruction? What's going on? First of all, if I read the text correctly, the Bible is trying to tell us by way of this story that America is not invincible or indestructible. Look at all these people who are gathered in this house. Whether it's Peter's house in Capernaum or some other's house is insignificant and inconsequential to me. What is important is this house represents people who are diseased, people who are sick, people who are infirm, people who are in need of wholeness, people who recognize their vulnerability, and people who recognize their destructibility. That's why the friends of the paralytic bring him to Jesus, because only Jesus can make crooked ways straight. Only the Lord can make rough places smooth. And whether we want to admit it or not, it takes this kind of a tragedy to make America realize that she is not whole. There's something broken about the nation. We have lived with an arrogance that has given us a false sense of superiority. And we honestly believe—yes, we do, black and white, red and yellow—we believe here in America that we are better than other people. We believe that we are better than Africa, better than Europe, and better than Asia. We believe that there never has been and never will be again a nation like the United States of America.

And we have learned the art of using capitalism to our greatest advantage. Why do you think they struck the World Trade Center first? Because it represents our economic wealth and capitalism. Anybody who ever looks at Wall Street recognizes that it's a dog-eat-dog, capitalist world. Insider-trading, companies buying out weaker companies. Ever since we got a new president we have been concerned about a recession. Every day, people look at what the stock market has to say and what the NASDAQ has to say. Well, the terrorists hit us—listen to me—at the point of America's god. America's god is not the God of Abraham, Isaac, and Jacob. America's god is capitalism. America's god is money. We will do anything to feather our nest, and we'll jump into bed with anybody who will help us feather our nest because we have had the erroneous belief that we are invincible and indestructible.

But did Tuesday teach us what should we walk away recognizing? Look at what happened when the Japanese bombed Pearl Harbor in 1941. The number of dead on that day was only 2,400 people. Three years later in 1944, D-Day, when the shores of Normandy were invaded, 1,500 dead. But in a matter of less than fifty-five minutes, five thousand died in the World Trade Center. Somewhere around eight hundred will be numbered among those dead in the Pentagon. Two hundred sixty-some died on four airliners. Somewhere near six thousand people, in less than sixty minutes. God's trying to tell us something. God doesn't care about Wall Street; God doesn't care about the Dow Jones; God doesn't care about the NASDAQ. God wants to know, "If my people will call upon my name and humble themselves and pray, turn from their wicked ways, then will I hear their prayers and I will heal their land." No, America is not the cat's meow. America is not a bag of chips and a bowl of dip. We are a nation like anybody else with a history of faith. And every now and then, when you get too big for your britches, God has strange ways of humbling us.

Not only do we discover that we are not invincible and indestructible but, my brothers and sisters, we also recognize that God is calling the nation to repentance. Look at the text. Jesus would not heal the man, he would not deal with his paralysis, until first the man's sins were forgiven. Now there's a prelude to forgiveness, and it's called repentance. How can God forgive us if there is not a willingness on our part to repent? And it might be that chickens have come home to roost in America. What's done in the dark will one day come to the light. The Bible puts it this way: "Whatsoever a man soweth." Let me rephrase that: Whatever a nation soweth that shall the nation also reap.

Let me deal with that on three frontiers. How many times have we heard folks singing "God Bless America"? That must be a strange song to the ears of God. These people are asking me to bless them, and in their Constitution they wrote back in 1787 on the separation of church and state. Strange music to God's ear. They want me, God, to bless America and back in the '50s they decided that they wanted to take prayer out of the schools. God bless America? They don't even want their football players to call on my name before they play ball. They want God to bless America. Yes, we always want God to bless us in tragedy. But we don't care about God in prosperity, when everything is going well. When peace is within our walls, to hell with God! But America's just like you and just like me. That's why a whole lot of you are here today who normally wouldn't be in church. I'm glad to see you! But all you Negroes wouldn't have church on your mind had there not been tragedy on Tuesday. Tragedy will drive you to the house of God and to the throne of grace. Somebody asked the Reverend Billy Graham, "Where was God?" "Oh, he was sadly on the fringe watching us." Somebody said, "Why is God on the fringe?" Rev. Graham said, "Because that's where we put him." We politely told God, "You stand over there until we tell you we want you." America has sins that need to be forgiven.

A lot of us don't want to admit it, but we have been a dirty nation. I remember back in the 1960s when Patrice Lumumba was wiped out in the Congo; that was done with American intelligence. We can be a dirty nation. When Salvador Allende was assassinated in Chile in South America, we were responsible for taking him out. We can be a dirty nation. How many years have we tried to assassinate Fidel Castro in Cuba without success? How many times have we tried to take out Mouammar Khadhafi without success? How many times have we tried to kill Saddam Hussein without success? And have you forgotten about Iran contra? Iran now is our enemy, but back yonder we gave refuge to the Shah of Iran. Oliver North led all of that mess that went on during Ronald Reagan's administration; arms for hostages was the Iranian debacle. It's been interesting to me that nobody wants to admit and nobody has said that we created Osama bin Laden. Many of you have forgotten, but we trained the people in Afghanistan to be terrorists. When we were in the Cold War against Russia, we trained them to be terrorists because they furthered our interests in trying to bring down the evil empire. But then we got friendly with Russia and forgot whom we had trained. Some of you all better watch whom you train. You better watch to whom you give your secrets. That stuff can come back to haunt you.

You know what blows my mind? And it's unfair. After the bombing of Pearl Harbor, we corralled Japanese and put them in camps, and now there are people in America who want to do evil against Arabs. There's something wrong. We want to raise hell about the Arabs, and nobody wants to talk about homegrown terrorists. We have grown terrorists right here on our own soil. Who was Timothy McVeigh? Who was Terry Nichols? Arabs didn't blow up the Federal Building in Oklahoma City; white Americans did! Arabs didn't shoot up that high school in Columbine; young white children did it! A high school in Jonesboro, not blown up by terrorists. We want to talk about how mean the Arabs are. We're growing terrorists, black and white! Many of our African American young people are terrorists. You are a terrorist when you have a violent mentality. You are a terrorist when crime is the main thing on your mind. I'm not going to let our community off. It's not safe to walk in our own communities anymore. We'll steal from each other; we'll cuss each other out, and many of us will do it to people who love us.

What's going on? The nation is not invincible; the nation is not indestructible; the nation needs to repent for the forgiveness of its sins. What's going on? In the final analysis, whether we want to admit it or not, we need God! That's why all those people were in that house in Capernaum—

because they needed God. That's why the paralytic's friends brought him to Jesus—because they needed God. That's why the president had enough sense to go to the Washington Cathedral on Friday and call for a national day of prayer—because he understands, we need God! We cannot heal ourselves, we cannot save ourselves, we cannot redeem ourselves, we cannot help ourselves, we cannot deliver ourselves, and we cannot justify ourselves! Only God can do that! Somebody ought to say "There is a God."

Let me tell you the fundamental mistake that America has made. The height and epitome of her arrogance got to her, and we have made the erroneous assumption that, because we are great, we will always be great. This doesn't have anything to do with the Bible; all you got to do is read history. Do you know what a season is? All you running around here talking about "This is my season"—no season lasts forever. We've had our season for prosperity. We've had our season without inflation, our season without recession. Do you know any nation that's been great forever? May I just do a quick roll call? Egypt, Babylon, Persia, Rome, Greece, France, Germany, England, Russia, America! Only a season and you better enjoy it while you can. What makes us think that we can beat the odds? Read Arthur Toynbee's *A Study of History.* Read Edward Gibbons's *The Rise and Fall of the Roman Empire,* and you will discover that once a nation begins to deteriorate when it comes to her ethics and her morals, she's on her way out. Look at our morals, look at our ethics—they are deteriorating. Things that used to raise the eyebrow don't raise the eyebrow anymore. Almost anything goes! Our sexual mores have changed. People now snuff out life by murder and don't care what the consequences are. Listen to the music our children are singing! We're destroying ourselves and we think we're going to live forever.

What's going on? The plane crashes outside of Pittsburgh, and it is now believed the destination for that plane was the Capitol. The Capitol where the House of Representatives reside, the Capitol where the Senate resides. If the plane had hit the Capitol, in one instant, the whole United States government would have been wiped out. Which means that if we had no government, we would have been ripe for invasion! No government—that [would have] left the president and the Supreme Court in charge. I don't know about you, but I don't want to be in the hands of

Mr. Bush and the Supreme Court because they have already shown what they think about people like me.

Oh, my brothers and my sisters, all of you who have the John Wayne mentality. I was in the barbershop yesterday, these young ignorant brothers getting haircuts and they've got no sense in their head. I can't stand stupidity. I mean, if you don't have anything intelligent to say, shut up! They said, "You know the Muslim Arabs, you know, just drop bombs on them, just blow them up!" I had to sit there and listen to wholesale ignorance, mammoth stupidity. I know it ain't that easy. This ain't World War I, this ain't the Korean War, this ain't Vietnam. We're not just talking about SCUD missiles in the Persian Gulf. This is war twenty-first century style! We're talking about nuclear war. We're talking about biological and chemical warfare. Oh yes, something ought to be done. I'm not saying we ought to roll over and play dead, but Jesus said that if you live by the sword you gonna die by it. God's already said, "Vengeance is mine. I *will* repay."

Listen, just listen. If we make a calculated effort, in terms of the wrong decision, we literally could inaugurate Armageddon. The Arabs control the British reservoir of oil. We ain't talking about your little jive car and folk running to the pumps, gassing up. We're not talking about the oil you need to keep your house warm in the wintertime. If those Arabs decide to cut off oil and form a blockade around it, ain't no jets gonna fly, ain't no bombs gonna fall. So what I'm saying is there's got to be, as Paul said, a more excellent way. No, no, this ain't the time to go to Camp David and sit around and just strategize militarily. No, no, we need to be in the Washington Cathedral every day. You all better pray for the president; he's listening to four voices—Vice President Dick Cheney, Secretary of Defense Donald Rumsfeld, National Security Advisor Condoleeza Rice, and Secretary of State Colin Powell—and all of them are military minded. There's nothing wrong with that, but at some point, God's got to step in.

I wonder today if there's anybody here who believes God still speaks. How many of you know God still speaks in the midst of chaos? Can I tell you what I really believe? Can I tell you why I believe America still lives and why God still has mercy on America? I believe God still has mercy on America because of black people. We know what it is to go through hell. We know what it is to go through a holocaust and survive. We know what it is to have jumbo jets hit us in our economic pockets, in our political pockets, and in every other pocket and still rise like a phoenix out of the ashes. I believe America is still alive because there are black people who know how to call on the name of God. And I need somebody in here today who is not ashamed to call on the name of God. Somebody in here needs to be able to say, "I've seen the lightning flashing and heard the thunder roll; I've felt sin's breakers dashing, trying to conquer my soul. But, I heard the voice of Jesus, telling me still to fight on."

I wonder, does anybody believe it? He promised never to leave me, never to leave me alone. Oh yes, we ought to sing "God Bless America," but when we get through, somebody better sing, "I need thee, oh, I need Thee! Every hour, I need thee." We ought to sing "The Star Spangled Banner," but when we get through somebody ought to sing, "My faith looks up to thee, thou Lamb of Calvary, Savior divine! Lord, hear me while I pray...." I thank God for "The Battle Hymn of the Republic," but once that fades away, somebody ought to be able to get up, somebody ought to be able to cry out, "My hope, my hope, my hope is built on nothing less than Jesus and his righteousness. I dare not trust the sweetest frame, but only lean on Jesus' name. On Christ, the Solid Rock I stand, all other ground is sinking sand." Jumbo jets are sinking sand. The World Trade Center is sinking sand. The Pentagon is sinking sand. The White House is sinking sand. The president is sinking sand. The Congress is sinking sand. The Senate is sinking sand. But I know somebody who stood before the World Trade Center. Yeah, yeah, yeah! I know somebody who is going to stand when the smoke clears and the dust settles. He'll still be there!

Alert When He Comes

Delores Carpenter

September 16, 2001

Blessed are those slaves whom the master finds alert when he comes; truly I tell you, he will fasten his belt and have them sit down to eat, and he will come and serve them." —Luke 12:37, NRSV

Myy subject this morning is "Alert When He Comes." When tragedy hit on Tuesday, I wonder how alert we all were. Or were we totally oblivious? I called one person to tell her Howard University had closed; she hadn't heard a thing about it. It's amazing how we can't see danger coming. It's amazing how, so often, even our Central Intelligence Agency can be caught off guard because they're not alert. Because we're not watching. We knew for many years that terrorism was a great possibility in this country. I remember going to Andrews Air Force Base on a regular basis, and often there was extra security. They'd be under a security alert, and the alert was always for terrorism. And I guess the question is, How is it that with all the security of airlines and even of our military, why is it we didn't see this coming? Why is it that we had no warning? Well, I would contend it's because people weren't alert as they should have been. We're becoming more alert. I hope we do not go back to the way we were; you know we've got to take precautions. And it's a good thing because when we don't fear nothing and nobody, anything can happen to us. The Bible says that the beginning of wisdom is the fear of the Lord. Now if we fear what earthly men can do to us, how much more should we fear God, the one who can destroy both body and soul? If we have to be so alert in the natural earthly realm, how much more alert should we be about the heavenly realm? How much more alert are we going to be when Jesus comes? If we would change our lifestyle today because of what has happened—and we will change our lifestyle—then how much more should we be willing to change our lifestyle for the Lord? In today's passage, we are in the middle of Jesus' preparing his followers for a precarious future, material or otherwise. In verse 22, Jesus tells them not be to anxious about food, clothing, health, or their bodies. He tells them that God will see them through. In verse 32, he reiterates his exhortation not to be anxious, "Fear not little flock," and then he tells them to prepare for action.

You know, if we are going to be alert for God, we are going to have to move some things out of our lives. Amen? God is going to have to strip us of some of the things that occupy our time, our money, and our attention. Because the kingdom of God is drawing near. The disciples were urged to dispose of all of their possessions and to get ready. Those possessions can weigh you down. Amen? You ever had so many things that it just slows you down? You know if I could travel lighter and live more simply, I could get more done. How much clutter do you have in your life, in your home, in your closet? You know how many clothes you have. You got so many decisions to make when you go to the closet or when you go to do this or that. If you could just move out some of those things so that you could be ready! Be on a readiness assignment.

"At first the servants were alert and waiting for the return of the bridegroom from the wedding feast." Jesus now switches to the parable of the householder being alert for the coming of a thief, and in both cases he says our need is to be alert and to be ready. Now because two thousand years have come and gone with no ending of the present age, no breaking in of the kingdom of God, we might not feel the same urgency that the apostle Paul felt, because he thought Jesus would come at any moment. The early Christians didn't marry because they said there wasn't any point. Jesus was coming. They didn't horde up things; they didn't store up things; they didn't make long-range plans. Why? Because Jesus was coming back.

Maybe Jesus hasn't come back, but you've got to live every day as though he's coming today. He may be coming today. You step outside this church, he may come now. We may not get out of here this morning for he is soon to come and sooner than we think. We must live our lives on tiptoed expectancy that he is coming any minute. We still need to be alert and watching for the kingdom. This gives us hope and inspires us to do what the Lord has called us to do. It's like when your parents go away and leave you home. You figure you've got all day to clean the house. You don't always get up and hurry. But when time comes, you know Momma and Daddy are coming home, you get real busy cleaning up cooking and everything, trying to be ready. Why? Because you're alert. You've got to get a job done, but you ought not to wait until the last minute. Every day may be the last minute. This may be my last time. I don't know. Tuesday could have been the last day.

Well, I know a little bit about that, being a cancer survivor since 1983. I had stage three out of four breast cancer. I learned in that experience that I had to get up and work while it's day because I don't know when night is coming. They told me that if I lived five years, that's what they call cured. If you're "cured," you've only got five years. Now, some people when they heard this, they might go home, put their feet up, and take good care of themselves. But when I heard this might be my last time, I got busy doing the Master's will.

I would never have been a pastor if it had not been for cancer. I'd been preaching for twenty years and was ready to retire. But when cancer came I got busy. I forgot about retirement. This may be my last time. I don't know. I remember one night I was a fill-in for Dr. Sam Proctor. Because Dr. Proctor was coming, the church was packed. All the preachers were there from all over the Baltimore area and Dr. Proctor asked me would I go in his place, and I was shaking in my shoes. I remember what Dr. Marion Basker said. I said, "Dr. Basker, I don't know what I'm going to do. All these people who come tonight to hear Dr. Proctor instead will hear me." He said, "Delores, preach like a dying woman to a dying congregation." You know we ought to preach every sermon as though it is our last sermon, and we ought to listen to every sermon as though it is our last sermon, because Jesus said, "Get ready." You know, T. D. Jakes wasn't the first one to say, "Get ready. Get ready. Get ready." Long before Bishop Jakes said, "Get ready," Jesus said it.

Jesus said, "Blessed are those who the master finds alert," awakened, fully awake. You know, there's a difference between just being here and being alert. Some people are in a daze. Some people are the walking dead. Some of them, you're looking at them, you're talking to them. They don't respond to anything. They don't hear anything you're saying. Their mind is miles away. They aren't alert. When you're alert, you're watching.

The criminal knows that you're lax. That you're careless. That you're indifferent. That you're apathetic. And it works the same way spiritually. Satan knows when you're tending to your spiritual house and when you're just being lackadaisical. You've got the door open, you let anything come in.

Also, notice the watch words of Jesus: "Do not be afraid in the end time." That's so important for us to hear today. Fret not yourself because of this evil that has come upon us. And our hearts go out to everyone who's suffering today, especially those people in New York walking the streets with pictures of their loved ones. It breaks my heart to see that. One of the children in our youth center was on one of those planes, an eleven-year-old—on her way to a field trip with a teacher to California. Think of the people in California who were trying to get home, and never got home. Think of the fact they'll never find some of those bodies. They may plow through that stuff for weeks, but after awhile they've got to bulldoze the rubble out of there. Body parts will not ever be identified and loved ones are going to have to be remembered with a memorial service and families will never get the remains of their loved ones.

But, in spite of all of this tragedy that has happened, how afraid are we of God? Now you'll be very afraid of planes and buildings going down after seeing those firefighters being suffocated to death under that ash. But do we have the same fear that God can destroy both body and soul?

The fall of the stock market, loss of our jobs, our health insurance, and even our car insurance will get us upset. The loss of health, we worry about that. You know, I'm getting near retirement age and worried about if I'm going to be real healthy. I don't want to retire and be sick. I don't want to retire and be poor. I tell people I don't want to outlive my money or my friends. If you don't have enough to think about to depress you, just turn on *60 Minutes* tonight or open the newspaper today and you'll find a reason to fear.

We live in an anxious world, and thus we must listen to what Jesus is saying. As the Lord was comforting the fearful people of his day, he taught us about turning our eyes away from our fears and towards the coming of the great kingdom that he talked about. Jesus lived it, he died for it, and he rose again to rule over it.

And my question for the church is this: Why are we not enthusiastic and alert and ready for action in our churches? I don't know about you, brother pastor. Maybe everybody here is anxious, alert, and ready to work. But where I pastor in Washington D.C., there's a whole lot of apathy. And one of the answers to the question of why we are not alert is that we are just tired. We're tired. But not in the good way, because there's bad tired and there's good tired. What do I mean by "bad tired"? Bad tired comes from feeling like what you do doesn't make a difference. Part of why we're not working is we don't think we matter or that what we do counts, or even some of us think the more we try to do the worse things get. We call that the Reverse Midas Touch. Rather than everything turning to gold, everything turns to something else—even the things we try to do for Jesus. Psychologists call this learned helplessness. Learned helplessness. We get real tired 'cause it just seems like we can't make a difference. And when you feel that way, then you're not ready for action and instead you're always ready to quit, always ready to throw in the towel. I wonder why, even in the church, if someone looks at you the wrong way, you're ready to quit. One little thing goes wrong, we're ready to give up so quickly.

A man went to preach in New England. He was a missionary and God told him preach a sermon titled "Rise Up, O Men of God." When he got up there, he said, "Lord, I don't know because I see some little old ladies up in here." Wasn't a man in sight. "Rise Up, O Men of God"? But he was obedient to God, and he preached that sermon anyway. He talked about the hills of Africa where he saw some of the villages that had never heard of Jesus Christ. And he was telling the ladies, "I want you to go. We need people to come and go to Africa, and preach the gospel of Jesus Christ." So he did what God told him, sat down, felt bad. You know, sometimes when we work for the Lord, we don't get immediate gratification. You don't have people complimenting you all the time, congratulating you all the time. So he felt a little discouraged; he sat down. But a little boy he hadn't seen during the service came to him. In those days the organ was in the balcony and the little kid was so small, and the organ was so big, that he couldn't even see him. But he came up and he said to the preacher, "Do you think I'm good enough for Africa?" That little boy turned out to be David Livingston, one of the greatest medical missionaries to the continent of Africa who has ever lived. You never know how God is going to use you. That's why you need to be alert. Amen!

Jesus said: "Watch and pray. Yea, don't put your hand to the plow and turn back." I'm steady, steady, steady with Jesus because when I need somebody to steady me, he's there for me. If he's there for me, I'm going to be there for him. I can tell it's going to take more than alarm clocks to wake us up, to fire us up. It's going to take Jesus filling us up with hope, restoring us with hope, restoring hope into our weary hearts. A song says, "Jesus is a rock in a weary land." For you to understand that song, you need to know it's written for desert people, and in the desert when that sun would be so hot, the only thing that could give shade was a rock. You got behind a rock to get out of the sun when the storm would come and the sand would blow and could kill you out there. You had to make your way to the rock so that the rock could protect you from the sand storm. Jesus is such a rock in a weary land. You may be weary, but if Jesus comes, he will wake you up. Fire you up. Get you up. Lift you up.

Looks like Jesus has come to wake us up. In this text he says, "Blessed are those slaves who the master finds alert when he comes. Truly, I tell you he (Jesus) will fasten his belt and have them sit down and eat and he will serve them." There is a mighty revelation in this text because what it is telling us is he doesn't just call us to serve him but he said, "I'll serve you. If you get a little tired, sit down a while and I'll serve you." Isn't that a wonderful thing? Why wouldn't you serve a God like that? When he got ready to die, he told the disciples, "Meet me in the upper room. Don't have to bring any money, just come like you are. I'll prepare the meal." Hallelujah. And he's been doing it ever since.

Oh, but how many of us know how to receive from the Master? Many of us are not receiving from God the things that God wants to give us.

Amen? Because we have been so busy asking God for what we want that we don't realize God wants to give us something different. You're so busy asking for what you want that you've missed this perfect will. I love the song that says "The safest place I know is in the center of his will, his perfect will," because I've learned that God has more for us than we can ever receive—surpassing all of our imagination and all of our asking. So, I got tired of asking him for things, and I just said, "God whatever you're willing to give me, I'm willing to receive."

This text says that he will come and he'll tell you to sit down and he will serve you. That's a great meal. "I prepare a table before you in the presence of your enemies." Glory. Hallelujah. "I will set the menu for you. Sit down and rest a little while." See, it's a two-way street. I don't just work with him but he comes alongside of me.

You know the old saints used to say: "Prop me up on every leaning side. Strengthen me where I'm weak, Lord." And God will do that. Just when you are most tired, he'll come along and give you that second wind. Have you ever been exercising and you thought you were going to pass out and all of a sudden a second wind comes? You can go faster now. Jesus is that second wind. He'll send the Holy Ghost {who} will give you a second wind. Then I run on a little harder and go farther than I thought because he's my coach and he tells me, "Come on. You can do it if you try. Don't give up. Don't stop. Don't look back. Just keep coming. I'll take your hand. If you get a little hungry, rest for a while. I'll give you food to eat. I'll give you water springing up to everlasting life." What a mighty God we serve!

We are not alert because we feel tired, and second, we are not alert because we forget how beautiful the destination of our reward, how marvelous is our salvation. You know some of us got saved so long ago it doesn't excite us anymore this place called heaven, this place called the kingdom of God. Well, let me talk about it this way. How many of you went on vacation this summer, raise your hand? I had a joyous summer. I saw some beautiful places. But you know when you're on vacation what are you doing— planning for the next vacation, right? While you're there, you're thinking about all the other places you want to be. I don't know about you but I got all kinds of vacation books on my table. In fact, I've got my trip to the Grand Canyon already planned for next year, and I can already imagine I'm going to have a good time. See, I don't have to get there to have a good time. I just have a good time thinking about getting there. Amen? Hallelujah! When you've got expectancy, you just have fun looking forward to having fun. You do more talking and planning about what you're going to do, and sometimes you enjoy that more than the event.

Well, I want to tell you God told Abraham that he had a new home for him. Amen. Abraham and many other people in the Bible, they desired a better country that is a heavenly home. Hebrews 11:16 [says] that they believed that God was preparing a heavenly city for them. The key to living a marvelous life in Christ is to trust what God says in the Word is true and to believe that God has a wonderful place for us, a heavenly home, a place more wonderful than any vacation spot. Better than Spain, Hawaii, and Grand Canyon all rolled into one. But, sometimes I think we act like we are more excited about our vacation plans than our eternal plans.

And friends, we do not have to wait until we get to heaven to sit at the table with Jesus. One of my favorite parts of Scripture is when God came down on Mt. Sinai and the people came to the bottom of the mountain, and God said, "Moses, you and the elders. Come on up to the mountain." And God Almighty sat down in the middle of them that night and had a holy communion with Moses and the elders. One of the first holy communions in the Bible. And we see God communing with his people again and again and again, because there's food that he wants to give you. Not the manna that the ancestors ate and then were hungry again. But he said, "I want to give you food that's called everlasting life. Not water from a well; you drink it and you get thirsty again, but I want to give you water that will never deplete. You'll never thirst again." He said, "Oh, if you're thirsty, come and you don't have to bring any money." Aren't you glad it's free? Hallelujah. Oh, I'm glad about it today. If you had to pay for it, I might not have the price, but he said, "Come on without money. Eat at my table." When I'm hungry, he feeds me. When I'm thirsty, he leads me beside still waters; he restores my soul. Goodness and mercy follow me all the days of my life, and that's why I dwell, I dwell, I dwell, in the house of the Lord all the days of my life.

If you're here this morning and you're not ready for action, get yourself ready. Keep your eye on heaven and then let God come alongside you.

Somebody said, He's Emmanuel with us. The yoke is easy and the burden's light, because you don't have to make this journey all alone. He'll come beside you. He'll hold your hand. He'll lift your head. Somebody knows what I'm talking about.

And somebody this morning needs to respond. Drag your emptiness. Drag your tiredness. Drag your powerlessness. Drag it on to Jesus so that he can sit you down and he can serve you. Somebody said, "What's he gonna serve? What's on the menu?" I think there's going to be some love on the menu. I believe there's going to be some forgiveness on the menu. Hope has got to be on the menu—a new vision for a new day, after the rubble is cleared. Drag ourselves to Jesus. Let him remind us he's still with us, that he will never leave us, and he will plant our feet on higher ground.

"On Christ, the solid Rock, I stand. All other ground is sinking sand." Then, after he picks you up and fixes you up, then he sends you on your way in the Great Commission to do what he taught us to do—to serve, to serve. Aren't you glad this morning? Didn't he wake you up? You said he woke you up this morning, but are you awake? Are you alert? Are you watching?

Oh, I'm so glad he came into my life. I'm so glad he wasn't a tourist. He wasn't cruising through my neighborhood. I'm glad he wasn't just making a pop-in call. But, I praise him because he took up residence. Glory in my heart. He said, "I'm going to stay with you always." If you're fearful, if you're depressed, he'll give you joy. Hallelujah. If you're down, he'll raise you up. Yes, he will.

What Have I Left?

Michael Eric Dyson
SEPTEMBER 16, 2001

I want to say [thank you] to Congresswoman Barbara Lee. [When I heard about the vote,] I leaned over to Dr. Wilson and I said, "Is she really *the* only person in the United States Congress to stand up against the machinery of war and vote 'No'?" And at a time, be reminded, when our sentiments and passions have been shaped by the media to make us believe that the only alternative is to stick that colossal military foot on the necks of people throughout the world without trying to negotiate—which is the reason why we left Durban, [South Africa,] and couldn't even talk at the table at the World Conference on Racism. This is the same government that refuses to acknowledge your pain and the domestic terrorism that we confront on a daily basis in Watts, Oakland, Harlem, and Detroit. The same government that refuses to stop racial profiling and police brutality—that's terrorism, too. And now we, as people of color, are being seduced into believing that the only alternative is to do to them what has been done to us, to bomb them as they have bombed us.

So I want to thank Congresswoman Barbara Lee for her bravery and for her courage. God bless you. Because we ain't trying to act like bin Laden is our buddy. He started off in Africa. We ain't stupid. But we're caught in the midst of this. American imperialism and colonialism is an old tradition.

In fact, America trained bin Laden as part of the Afghanistan movement against the Soviet Union. The CIA, the Central Intelligence of America, trained him to do battle. Now he turns that weaponry on America. Don't hate the player, hate the game.

Oh, America's got a short memory. Not to suggest we don't have to have a strategic response to terrorism throughout the world. Of course we do. But the question is how will we hold ourselves accountable for creating the conditions where folks in Palestine are clapping when they hear about America [being attacked]? Don't get it twisted, see, because Negroes were clapping when O.J. got off. White America thought we had lost our minds. We ain't thought O.J. was innocent; we just didn't believe he was guilty. Because we have been trying to tell America for years: you can't mistreat people in an unjust system and expect us to celebrate the way in which you've hurt us. So when O.J. came along, we knew he was perfect for white America. O.J. was a substitute white man in American society. There wasn't nothing black on him but the bottom of his shoes. But since they loved him, that was our time to say, "Yeah, this is wrong and we're glad the brother got off because you didn't prove your case."

Now, when we see these brothers and sisters in Palestine, every day they listen to America refusing to be balanced in its telling of the story about Palestine and Israel. Every day the infantry is reported on as a bunch of rebellious thugs who in defense of their own country refuse to concede authority to Israel. We ain't hating on Israel. We don't drink "Hate-orade." We are peaceful people, but don't be player hating on the Palestinians. Don't not tell their side of the story. Let's talk about balanced reporting and the need to give history and perspective to all of the warfare going on in the Middle East. They are our brothers and sisters as well.

And so, yes, we need to respond to terrorism, but we have to be responsible for the way in which we are a part of a nation that has hurt other people in the name of democracy. And we know we've been mad at America, too. And still be mad. Right? Because as soon as all of the unity fades away in the face of the love, affirmative action still ain't getting passed. Reparations by Condoleeza Rice, *your* representative of national security in the Bush administration, will still be put down.

So my point is, yes, we are American, but we've being telling America we've been American from the beginning. And if you're really American, you ought to tell the truth about America. Loving America doesn't mean uncritically celebrating everything she does. If Martin Luther King Jr. said "I love America enough to tell her the truth," and the truth is we've been wrong, then we've got to deal with that as well. It ain't just bin Laden; it's the "been lying" we've been doing and now we've got to straighten that up, too.

And, see, this book I just wrote on Tupac [Shakur], that's another young brother who was subjected to the American media trying to dis' him. But Tupac dropped science. Long before racial profiling became an issue, he was talking about that, talking about police officers getting paid to beat up on blacks, talking about his taxes going toward paying those same cops. And he didn't say "nigger." He said, "Nigga." N-i-g-g-a—Never Ignorant Getting Goals Accomplished. Don't get it twisted.

So one of the things black youth culture helps to remind us is the degree to which America will descend to try to denigrate our identity. Tupac was telling the truth about that. Yeah, he might have been cussing, but that ain't the first cuss word you've heard. And what's more profane and vulgar, saying "m—f—" or treating somebody like one? So you've got hip-hoppers with their jeans slung way down low to their behind who are talking about stuff, but really acting like love because they're selling wolf tickets. Or, you have an American government with suit and tie that will blow to smithereens its enemies without compunction and refuse to acknowledge its own perpetuation of global domination of white supremacy. That's the reality we must always confront. Thank God for the hip-hoppers who tell the truth about that.

Let's look now at our text from Judges 18:24, from the Revised Standard Version: "And he said, 'You take my gods which I made, and the priest, and go away, and what have I left? How then do you ask me, What ails you?'" I just want to preach a bit about, "What have I left?"

In Ephraim's hill country, the central highland of Palestine, the site of so much controversy and confusion today, a woman had saved eleven hundred shekels or pieces of silver and that amounted really to her life's savings. That was a whole lot of cheddar for those times. And she saved it up and accumulated it over years of hard work and extracting her savings and the dowry she might have inherited to create her little personal fortune. And one day somebody stole that personal fortune. All of the accumulated wealth that she had managed to sock aside was now depleted by a barbaric act of thievery. And so—like many of us whose wealth is depleted by a singular act of extraordinary degradation and depravity—she cursed (with a holy curse, we're told) the folk who stole her money. She said, "Curses be upon those who have taken my money."

Money is always more than money. Currency is a symbol of an accumulated wealth that will never altogether be exhausted by the currency that symbolizes it. That's why they're always making arguments about do we have gold in Fort Knox to back up the money we've got circulating. Because the currency you hold is no better than the accumulated wealth that it symbolizes. You can have a whole lot of checks, but if you ain't got no money in the bank, the checks ain't really worth nothing. Now that don't stop some of us from still using them, but that's another sermon! Money is really always altogether more than money. It symbolizes how we relate to one another. It is a token of how we create relationships with one another. At the root of so much of the fratricide and the genocide in our world is the question of the use or abuse of money and wealth.

That's why when we talk about prosperity, it should always be within the context of God's plan. God is not interested in the unfettered, uncritical accumulation of wealth for self-aggrandizing purposes, for self-absorbed, narcissistic me-ism. It's about helping black folk. It's about helping this nation. It's about helping Africa. It's about helping our people.

And so she cursed those people who had stolen her money. Her son, Micah—which means "he who is like God"—turned out to be the person who is most shaken by her curse. Micah, whom she had reared with intense attention to nurturing in him the spirit of truth and of godliness, was shaken by that curse. Micah was convicted by her curse. He was convicted because he had stolen his mama's money.

How our children sometimes disappoint us. Of course, she probably would have said, "You didn't have to steal it. You could've asked me for it and I'd've gave it to you." I know that's bad grammar but that's some serious theology. "I'd have given it to you. You didn't have to pilfer it. You didn't have to steal it. You didn't have to, in the cover of night, sneak into my tent and remove my accumulated wealth—the wealth that had we used wisely would not have only helped me, but you. But in deference to immediate gratification, you ripped off not only my money, but also your future." We do that 'cause we're shortsighted. But see, sometimes that shortsightedness is a real road to some revelation that we have to confront.

So Micah ripped off his mama, stole her purse, and then when she uttered that curse, something deep in him was convicted. (Thank God for training and rearing your kids in the way they ought to go, for planting something in them. It might not come out when you think it ought to, but sometimes the Word of God that you give to them will resound in them, maybe not now but later.) And so, Micah goes to his mama and he says, "Mama, I am the one that stole that money." And his mama is so overwhelmed that he's told the truth that together they decide what to do. So they invest about two hundred shekels of that money and take it to a silversmith to melt it down into a molten and graven image.

Now, the tricky part here is that the money that was stolen is now replaced and restored, and now it is melted down into an idol to worship God. They're on touchy ground there because idol worship in that ancient world is already a source of enormous strain and consternation with the real God. So idol worship already was on the wrong footing, and in acknowledgement of the blessing God, they do something to contradict the spirit of the God, who gave them the blessing to begin with—because that's how messy human relationships are.

So in light of that, they melt down the gold into a god, into a molten image, and Micah even hires his son. He sets up his son as the priest of the temple he establishes in his home, a shrine to God. But then, another priest comes along—an educated Levite priest. The Levite priest had some serious learning and so Micah says to him, "I want you to be my priest. I'll give you ten pieces of silver a year." That was some serious money back then. "I'll give you a place to stay and some food to eat and some nice clothes if you will be *my* priest." Not God's priest, not God's prophet, not God's servant, but *my* priest. And so, the Levite signs on and he begins to become the priest of Micah in their homemade shrine in their tent.

A few months later along comes the traveling, roaming Danite tribe.

The tribe of Danite, who is homeless. Ain't got no home, looking for a home, looking for the Promised Land. And part of what was going on in the Middle East then is what's going on now, people arguing over geography as destiny. As Ralph Emerson put it, "Trying to argue about whose land belongs to who." And when you're already in a land and people claim it to be their Promised Land, that's a problem with you because you've already got the land. And God ain't told you about the deed God might have given to them. But in the name of God, they claim to own your land.

And so the Danites see the beautiful shrine in the house of Micah. And they see that silver god shining there and they see the priest and they want both of them. And so they steal the shrine of god. At first the priest puts up a battle, but then they say, "What do you want? Do you want to be pastor of a church with one person, with four people, or do you want six hundred members in your congregation? Plus, we're going to pay you more and give you a better retirement package." He said, "See you, Micah. Got to get with the Danites."

And so the priest went with them. And you know Micah was deeply upset and he said, "Oh my God, what have they done?" So he got some of his villagers and took some knives and some sickles. You know they didn't have that much armament back then because they were victims of their enemies. And one of the tragedies of minority people in a majority situation is that they've got to borrow the very armament they use from their enemies. And so they took up arms and they went out against these six hundred Danites, and they said, "Give us our stuff back." And [the Danites] laughed at them. "What are you doing? Don't play with us. There are six hundred people out here and you've got about what, twenty-five people?" And Micah said, "You have taken my gods; you have taken the priest who is my personal priest and you have taken them. What have I left? And that's the reason I'm asking you to give them back. Why then do you ask me what ails me? That's what ails me."

That question that Micah asks is really a question that all of us have to come to. In the midst of devastation, what have I left? But if you examine it, it was an opportune time for them to really dig deep into the spiritual resources that God had given to them. Because, after all, if God is going to be God, you've got to get rid of your other gods. And sometimes God does a jack move on your gods, just rips them off; just uses your enemies to take them away from you. I know we don't like that, but you know what Paul Shearer said? "Real worship is bringing gods we've made to bow down to the God who made us." Oh, but what do we do? We attempt to make God bow down before our gods. Oh, we know how we create our own gods—our gods of materialism. We know some of us are worshiping bling bling. Some of us are worshiping platinum. Some of us are worshiping Lexus and Rolls Royce. Some of us are worshiping materialism.

Now we know we live in a world where we need to have some accumulated wealth. I ain't stupid. Right? And the problem with so many black people is that we ain't got wealth. We've got a whole lot of income, but no wealth. Right? See, if you've got some serious wealth, you ain't got to have much of an income 'cause your wealth is going to make money. Your money is going to make wealth. Your wealth is going to create wealth. If you don't go to work today, you don't miss nothing. But most of us miss work, miss money, miss meal. Right? "Oh yeah, I'm making $500,000, but ain't got no wealth created." And so black communities have been wealth poor. And because we've been wealth poor, the infrastructure of the ghetto economy means we have to engage in underground economy: illicit materials, thieving, thugging, macking, pimping, and whoring as opposed to creating entrepreneurial expertise to perpetuate wealth to pass on to our children and to our grandchildren.

Now you might not like it, but some of the best examples of wealth creation in the black community come out of the hip-hop community. I ain't just talking about P. Diddy. He says, "I ain't got to write rhymes, I write checks." But I'm talking about Master P down in New Orleans. This man has created extraordinary opportunity for the poor people in his community. And now *Forbes* magazine has to acknowledge his entrepreneurial genius. Maybe he should be teaching over here at the Wharton School or over here at Georgetown University. So I'm not against that. But what I am against is this kind of uncritical celebration of the goods and services and materials of life as if they are themselves the sign of God's blessing to you.

See, the problem with that is that, when you ain't got no goods, are you not blessed by God? When you ain't living like Big Willie, does that mean God has not blessed you? We have to be very careful about talking about how God blesses us—even in our theology when it says I was spared. I was supposed to be at the World Trade Center doing a book signing the day after it went down. And then, I was in Boston Monday night, could've been on that plane Tuesday morning. Some of my friends and family said, "God blessed you." And I said, "Yeah, hold on, I am blessed by God, but not because I was spared." What kind of theology is that? So the people who went down to their deaths were not blessed? Blessing is not determined by possession of material wealth or even by your life. Blessing is determined by your relationship with God. Blessing is determined by your consciousness to know you need God. Blessing is determined by your intimate contact with the Almighty. Whether you are dead or alive, you are blessed, if you have that.

We have all these theologies that just sanctify materialism. We're mad at Jay-Z for talking about all this stuff and we say that's problematic. But Jay-Z ain't never claimed to be no prophet nor no preacher nor no teacher from God. But we've got people in the pulpit across America and the globe saying that, if God has blessed you, you ought to have a certain amount of money in the bank automatically—and if you don't, you're not blessed by God. Yes, we need the accumulation of wealth. Yes, we need to leverage our authority so that we can get out of poverty. Ain't nobody sanctifying this poverty except a capitalistic system that wants to keep us poor. But don't get it twisted. Don't identify God with the things you possess. God is not your car, not your house, not your clothes, not your capital, not your jewelry, not your ice, not your platinum, not your record deal, not your book deal, not your title. God is God by God's self.

And so, sometimes God has to send the Danites to rip off your gods. And maybe God is telling America that you've been worshiping your power too long. You've been worshiping your nuclear capability too long. What is a nuclear bomb going to do to somebody who doesn't care whether he lives or dies? Which is why I study some of these kids in the ghetto, because some of them are like that, too. Ain't got nothing to lose. Don't care about you or themselves. That's why they're in love with death. So much of their music talks about death. You know, like they're addicted to death. They *are* addicted to death because they live in a death-dealing culture that sees them as nothing but thugs and throwaways, so they begin to wear proudly the labels they are given. "You call me a thug? Darn right I'm going to be a thug." So we live in a culture that refuses to acknowledge their legitimacy or their centrality as human beings.

And then it's not just the white supremacists and mainstream culture that do it. Black people do it, too, to our own kids because they *is* your kids. Yeah, you may be afraid of them and yeah, some of them are misled and misdirected and got devil all up in it. Ain't no doubt about that. But these are your children. And if you are only concerned about the accumulation of your wealth, wanting your priest, wanting your preacher and not God's priest and God's preacher, you'll have ministers preaching a gospel that will reproduce your wealth while the masses of black people are going down the drain, to hell in a hand basket.

And those young prophets begin to spring up like Tupac, like Biggie, like Nas, and they begin to tell. They begin to use words because all they have is words. They have no wealth. They have no accumulated capital. They're living in an enclave of civic horror called the ghetto and the slum and black people who are wanting to distance themselves from them because they're the wrong kind of niggers. They ain't our kind of niggers. They're project niggers. And I'll tell you why so many black folk are upset with the rap music: The wrong niggers have got the microphone. Them ain't the folks we want to speak for us: Snoop Dogg, Lil' Kim, Foxy Brown. I understand ya, I feel ya. But here's the point, when they were anonymous, nobody knew their names. Many of us were not concerned about their plight, predicament, and culture. So as a result of that, they feel no moral responsibility to accede to our wishes now that they're on their own, away from our help; they've managed to rise up. So now you want them to be responsible when you weren't responsible for helping them from the beginning. They feel that. Don't always just give scholarships to the A student. Be worried about the C and D students, too.

I ain't justifying sexism and patriarchy [and] homophobia. I am not justifying beating up on women, calling them nasty names, 'cause that stuff is evil and problematic and wrong. But it didn't just begin with hip-hop culture. In most Baptist churches this morning, you can't find a female sitting up on the pulpit. Right? Because we are practicing patriarchy. Ain't nobody calling you no bitch but they're treating you like one if they don't let you into the place of power. You mean to tell me that the black church, which is 75 to 80 percent female, can't be run by a female? God ain't blessed her? God said, "If you don't cry out, the rocks will cry out." You mean God can call a rock "Reverend" but not a woman? What kind of theology is that? God comes in whatever form God chooses to.

And so, Micah said, "You've taken away my gods and you've taken away my priest." I done had my private Reverend, Mr., Dr., Professor, and now you done taken him. And, not only did you take my god, you took my priest that helped me with my god, which may be a good thing. Because, if you are a priest on somebody's payroll, you've got to say what they want you to say. You've got to do what they want you to do. And the problem with too many of us is that we've got too many priests and prophets on the payroll. Can't speak truth to power.

Don't get me wrong. It's hard to speak truth to power because you know you like going up to the White House. I've been there and done that. You like being in the halls of power. They may not call you because you're a little bit too uppity, a little bit too Afrocentric, a little bit too black for them, a little bit too discourteous in the face of romantic idealization of power. And he's our friend. He is our friend, so you end up saying everything like he's said it. Because, you can't be a priest or a prophet on payroll. And if you are a priest on payroll, you've got to go to the National Cathedral and say it's all right to simply drop a bomb and commit war as opposed to saying, "Slow down. There ain't but one God. We understand domestic policy. We understand the political machinations of governmental authorities who are appointed to represent the people. But that not withstanding, there's somebody else's voice that's got to be up in the mix. That maybe we ought to slow down and do as Psalm 46 says, 'Be still and know that I am God.' And maybe the problem is God is whipping us by saying you have been worshiping at the altar of your supremacy, your superiority, your power, your terrorism throughout the world. Stop!"

But if you are a preacher on the payroll, you can't say that. If you want to be on C-Span next week, you can't say that; want to be on CNN, can't say that; want to be on Nightline, can't say that; want to write another book, can't say that; want to still make money on the lecture circuit, can't say that; want to deliver some more preachers, can't say that; can't go to the revival next week if the other preacher doesn't believe in that stuff. You can't say that, but you've got to say that 'cause the only payroll you should be worrying about is the payroll of God, the economy of the kingdom. That's why when you listen to most of these preachers, if you wake up and turn on the TV, Martin Luther King couldn't get up in their church. Right? Martin Luther King with his prophetic gospel saying what thus saith the Lord. The average church that's preaching this kind of gospel, he can't get up in there. Now King wasn't perfect, but King was powerful and prophetic and told the truth and bore witness to the truth of God. And he said it in season and out of season. He said it when white folk wanted to hear it; he said it when they didn't want to hear it. He said it when Negroes wanted to hear it; he said it when Negroes didn't want to hear it.

Your job as a preacher, as a priest, as a prophet is to deepen people's consciousness of God. It's to nurture their spiritual awareness. It's to lead them to be self-critical and to preach justice. That ain't easy—especially when you are pastoring black folks. You've got to love black folk enough not to be scared of them. Because black folk don't appreciate nobody scared of them. Right? But if you'd stand up and tell the truth about what you think, even if they don't agree with you, they're going to appreciate the fact that you're telling the truth.

And so that kind of gospel means we challenge our own xenophobia, our own homophobia, our own viciousness towards women. You've got to be unafraid of black people enough, and love them enough, to tell them the truth. And, yes, maybe we are doing something in our inner-city communities that needs to be reconstructed because we are killing each other. We've got to tell the truth about that. But we don't cave into white supremacy that tries to make us pawns to beat up other Negroes. A real prophet uses his or her education in defense of the best interest of the people by preaching prophetically to them.

You cannot afford to be on the payroll of anybody but God. And the reason is not because we're perfect, not because we have a direct pipeline to God, but because we are under judgment ourselves, if we do not preach the gospel. If we are not being responsible for what God has given to us, we are sinning ourselves. And that means we have to oppose the wisdom of the world. Sometimes, like Representative Lee, you've got to stand up by yourself. It looks like nobody else is going help you; nobody else is with you. Even your former allies think you're crazy for what you're doing. If God has told you to do it, you've got to stand up to it.

And then when Micah asked that question, "What have I left?"—oh, that's a good time. When your gods are destroyed and your priests have gone away that's on your private payroll, that's a good time to hear God. What you got left? Just you and God. But that's all right. Ain't no harm in that. See you done got rid of the unnecessary. You done got rid of the contention. You done got rid of the non-vital. You know what's left? Just you and your God. And when that's left, you've got everything left.

What have I left when my gods are gone? What have I left when my preacher is gone? Me and my Savior. Just a walk in the garden. I talk with him and I walk with him and he tells me I am his own. And the joy I share, my God, and the peace I know. I'll tell you what you've got left. You become a prisoner of the permanent. And when you become a prisoner of the permanent, that's God in you. No matter what buildings crumble, no matter what lies are told, no matter what opposes you, God is in you. That's what we have left: A love for our Lord, a love for our God, our Priest, and our Christ. Peace.

Piety and the Public Square

Robert M. Franklin

SEPTEMBER 18, 2001

This commentary was prepared for National Public Radio.

Since the tragedies of September eleventh, more and more Americans are searching for answers in religion. The president and other elected officials have been conspicuously pious. Congressional leaders resembled a local choir as they soulfully rendered "God Bless America." And firefighters and rescue workers sought and received blessings from the clergy. During times of stress and sorrow, many who wear their religious faith loosely wrap themselves more tightly in it. And it appears that even the wall separating church and state becomes more like an open gate that allows lots of personal piety to escape into the public square.

Consider the reasons for the current resurgence of interest in religion. First, religion provides rituals or familiar and predictable patterns of speech and action. Rituals like singing the national anthem and lighting candles help people to gently reassemble the broken pieces of their lives. Also, rituals connect people to the grand story that infuses ordinary reality with meaning and purpose.

Second, religion motivates and mobilizes service on behalf of others. Whether the Muslim practice of giving alms to the poor, or the Jewish tradition of Jubilee, or the Christian example of the Good Samaritan, authentic faith rolls up its sleeves and makes life better for other people.

Third, religion offers a story or a grand narrative in which people may insert their group and personal stories and thereby make sense and significance of their lives. For instance, European immigrants and African slaves found the exodus story of the Hebrew Bible a powerful way of re-telling their own experience of pilgrimage from slavery to freedom. Sacred rituals, service and story have been evident during the early phase of our national search for comfort, strength, and meaning.

But there is another dimension of authentic religious faith that should not be ignored. It is the challenge of reckoning with individual and national sin. This is the ethical moment in religion that compels humans to ask forgiveness from a God that demands justice and compels them to seek reconciliation with fellow humans.

Unfortunately, America demonstrated impatience with the process of moral accountability when we walked out of the World Conference on Racism a few weeks ago. By showing our backs to legitimately aggrieved people from the developing world, America forfeited precious moral currency and may have caused more offense than we ever intended. If the truth be told, Western nations have benefited from the suffering and sacrifice of nameless masses from countries most of us can't find on a map. They deserve to be heard and perhaps to receive an apology from affluent nations. Colin Powell could have said something like this and perhaps have expanded international understanding and good will. Instead, these nations were left with the impression that Americans are too arrogant or are too busy making money to care much about their grief and poverty. I wonder, will those who today seek personal comfort in the presence of God remain in that presence long enough to discover that the God of Abraham, Jesus, and Muhammad also expects honesty about personal and national sin, humility in the presence of victims, and accountable behavior in the future?

President Bush has done a good thing in inviting the nation, believers and nonbelievers alike, to a national period of mourning, memorial, and prayer. Now, he should invite the nation to journey beyond singing, prayer, and candle lighting to a national discussion of our global responsibilities, and opportunities for healing old wounds. This will require honesty, humility, and a strong resolve never to repeat the mistakes of the past.

The Day of Jerusalem's Fall

Jeremiah A. Wright Jr.

SEPTEMBER 16, 2001

Remember, O LORD, against the Edomites the day of Jerusalem's fall.
—Psalm 137:7, NRSV

Most of us are only familiar with the first six verses of Psalm 137. They contain the powerful and immortal words of a people who are in exile; words that have been made into anthems and sacred songs, both in North America and in Jamaica. Forty years ago when I was in college, our college choir sang Psalm 137: By the waters of Babylon. There, we sat down and wept when we remembered thee, O Zion. Two hundred years ago almost everybody in the Caribbean was singing the Jamaican version, "By the waters of Babylon. There we sat down and wept." The captives in Babylon asked the question, "How shall we sing the Lord's song in a strange land?" The captives in America answered that question by creating an entirely new genre of music, the spirituals. They sang sorrowfully, "Sometimes I feel like a motherless child, a long way from home." They sang thoughtfully, "Nobody knows the trouble I've seen, nobody knows but Jesus." They sang defiantly, "Oh, freedom! Oh, freedom! Oh, freedom over me, and before I be a slave, I'd be buried in my grave and go home to my God and be free."

To quote Dr. Martin Luther King Jr., "The African in exile took Jeremiah's question mark and streamed it out into an exclamation point." Jeremiah, who saw his people in exile, asked the question, "Is there no balm in Gilead?" The Africans who were in exile in a strange land said, "Oh yes, there is a balm in Gilead." The exiles in Psalm 137 asked the question, "How can we sing the Lord's song in a strange land?" The Africans exiled in America answered their question and said, "I sing because I'm happy. I sing because I'm free. His eye is on the sparrow, and I know he watches me."

Psalm 137 has inspired anthems, spirituals, poems, and sermons. Psalm 137 has inspired the hearts of millions as they have reflected on the beauty and splendor of the city of God, Jerusalem. "If I forget you, O Jerusalem, let my right hand forget her skill," the text says in Psalm 137:5. It means, "May my right hand become useless if I forget Jerusalem." The text goes further to say in verse 6, "Let my tongue, designed to sing praises, cling to the roof of my mouth if I do not remember you, O Jerusalem..."

Now in our class sessions on our church study trips, I have lifted up these verses to help our church members understand much of what it is they feel as they have stood in the slave castles in West Africa, as they have stood among the poverty in Ethiopia, stood in the townships of South Africa, and stared at the prevails in El Salvador, in Rio de Janeiro, and in Brazil. African Americans have a surge of emotions as they see the color of poverty in a world of wealth and begin to understand that it is no accident that the world's poor are one color, and the world's rich are another color. When they tie together the pieces of five hundred years of colonialism, racism, and slavery with what they see in 2001, a surge of emotions hits them and the last three verses of Psalm 137 help them understand what it is they are feeling. I have treated these verses in a classroom setting and on the study tours that our congregation has taken, but I have never touched them in a sermon. I was licensed to preach in May of 1959. I was ordained in January of 1967, and I became a pastor in March of 1972, but in all of my years of preaching, I have never preached a sermon which dealt with these difficult verses, these last three verses in Psalm 137. These verses are brutally honest and express what the people of faith really feel after a day of devastation and senseless death.

Today I was telling Freddie Haynes that the spirit of God has nudged me to touch upon [these verses] and to treat them prayerfully as many of us try to sort out what it is we are really feeling, and why it is we are feeling what we feel after the trauma and the tragedy of the attacks on the World Trade Center and the Pentagon, symbols of what America is—money and the military. Some of the feelings we have as people of faith in the twenty-first century are similar to the feelings the people of faith had in the sixth century B.C., and when you read and study this psalm in its entirety, the parallel between those feelings becomes almost eerily clear. That's why I didn't want you to stop at the famous and familiar verse 6. I wanted you to read, to hear, and to experience all nine verses of Psalm 137 to get the full scope of this psalm.

Turn in your Bibles to 2 Kings, the twenty-fifth chapter. In that chapter, there is a graphic description of the carnage and the killings that took place on the day of Jerusalem's fall. The King of Judah with all of his army fled. Verse 4, they tried to run but the army of the Chaldeans pursued the king, captured the king, and literally committed murder. Verse 7, they slaughtered and did senseless killings. They slaughtered the sons of Zedekiah, and made the king watch. Then they put out his eyes, so that would be the last thing he had any visual image of—like commercial airliner passenger planes slamming into two office buildings killing thousands, for no reason other than hatred. The psalmist says, "Remember, O Lord, against the Edomites the day of Jerusalem's fall."

Verse 8 of 2 Kings 25 says, "Nebuzaradan, captain of the guard, in the service of the Nebuchadnezzar, King of Babylon, came to Jerusalem, and burned." Now get this image clear. Burned. Get it in your mind. "He burned the house of the Lord." He burned the king's house. He burned all the houses of Jerusalem, every great house he burned down. "Remember, O Lord, against the Edomites the day of Jerusalem's fall." And all the army of Chaldeans, who were with the captain of the guard, broke down the walls of Jerusalem.

Now you've got to remember the real and the symbolic significance of the walls of Jerusalem. Our choir sings, "Great is the Lord and greatly to be praised in the city of our God." Jerusalem. "Let Mount Zion rejoice." Jerusalem. "Let the daughters of Jerusalem be glad." "Walk around Zion." That's Jerusalem. "Go around about her, count her towers, tell the towers, tell the towers thereof." The towers of Jerusalem were a visible symbol of her greatness, her power, and her invincibility. "Mark ye well her bulwarks; consider her bulwarks and consider her palaces." There is Jerusalem, invulnerable Jerusalem, invincible Jerusalem, and the city where God dwells. Jerusalem. The Chaldeans smashed and shattered that sense of security and invincibility when "a breach was made in the invincible walls." One side of the Pentagon was wiped out and the people who were in there, like the people who defended Jerusalem on that wall, were wiped out.

First there was a breach in the wall in verse 4, and then verse 10 it says, "They broke down all the walls of Jerusalem." They burned everything they could burn and took most of the people into exile. *Remember, O LORD, against the Edomites the day of Jerusalem's fall*. The symbol of power was gone. The substance of their military and monetary power was gone. The towers of Jerusalem were gone. It took eight years to build the World Trade Center. It took Solomon seven years to build a temple in Jerusalem with its towers, and within eight hours, it was gone. It took Solomon fourteen years to build his palace—the symbol of wealth, the symbol of magnificence, might, majesty—and within eight hours it also was gone.

The day of Jerusalem's fall was a day that changed these people's lives forever. The day of Jerusalem's fall was a day of pain, a day of anger, a day of rage, a day of terror, a day of outrage, a day of death, a day of destruction, and, verse 8 of Psalm 137 says, "a day of devastation." The people who sang this song in Psalm 137 saw their loved ones die. The people who sang this song saw the carnage. The people who sang this song saw their landmarks burned. They saw their church burned. They saw their town burned. They saw their places of employment burned. Some of the people they worked beside they would never see again. Some of the people they walked beside they would never see again. Some of the people they lived beside they would never see again. And the day of Jerusalem's fall was a day that would live forever in their memories. The day of Jerusalem's fall was a day that changed their lives forever. When you read this psalm of remembrance you can understand the words, "By the waters of Babylon we sat down and wept when we remembered Jerusalem."

When you read the song of remembrance, you see the people of God make three distinct moves. They move first of all from reverence. Those thoughts in Psalm 137 are thoughts of reverence. The memories of Jerusalem are memories of reverence. Jerusalem is where the house of God was. Reverence. Jerusalem is where the temple of Solomon was. Reverence. March about Zion, and go 'round about her. Reverence. The Lord is in his holy temple. Reverence. Isaiah said, "In the year that the King Uzziah died I saw also the Lord sitting on a throne high and lifted up. And the train of his garment of the hem of his robe filled the temple." Reverence. "The seraphim were in attendance above the Lord. Each had six wings." That's in Isaiah 6:2. "They covered their face with two. They covered their feet, and with the other two, they flew and called out one to the other 'Holy, Holy, Holy is the Lord of hosts; the earth is full, the whole earth is full of his glory.'" Reverence. Reverence was shown when Solomon prayed and asked God's blessing on the temple in Jerusalem. You know the story. Fire came down from heaven in 2 Chronicles 7, and the glory of the Lord filled the temple. The priests could not go in, and the people fell down and worshiped. Reverence. The thoughts of Jerusalem in Psalm 137 are thoughts of reverence. "If I forget you, O Jerusalem, let my right hand forget her cunning." Reverence. "Let my tongue cleave to the roof of my mouth if I do not remember you, Jerusalem." Reverence.

But keep on reading. The people of faith move from reverence in verses four to six to revenge. In versus eight and nine, they want revenge. They want somebody to destroy those who devastated them. In fact they want God to get even with those who did evil. *Remember, O LORD, against the Edomites the day of Jerusalem's fall*. The first move is when the people of faith moved from reverence to revenge.

The second move in this text is a move from worship to war. Jerusalem is where they worshiped. Now they have declared war. Let me put it another way. The second move is a move from the thoughts of paying tithes. Jerusalem is where the people of faith paid tithes. Solomon led the people of God in paying tithes at the temple in Jerusalem. Jerusalem. The temple of God, the house of God is where the people of God make sacrificial offerings to God way after the temple was restored and rebuilt. The temple in Jerusalem is the house of God where the people of God brought their tithes and their offerings. Jesus' mother and father brought him to the temple to present him to the Lord, and they brought a sacrificial offering.

Jerusalem. The temple, the house of God, is where the people of God paid tithes and sacrificial offerings to God. What does God, God's self say in Malachi 3:10? "Bring all the tithes into the storehouse that there may be meat in my house, the temple, and prove me now herewith." The second move now in Psalm 137: There's a move from the thoughts of paying tithes to the thoughts of paying back. O daughter of Babylon, you devastator. Happy, blessed shall they be, who pay you back for what you did to us. That's payback. The big payback.

Every public service of worship I have heard about so far in the wake of America's tragedy has had sympathy and compassion for those who were killed and their families and has asked for God's guidance upon the "selected" president and our war machines as they do what they do and what they "gotta do." Payback. There's a move in Psalm 137 from thoughts of paying tithes to thoughts of payback. A move if you will, from worship to war. A move, in other words, from the worship of the God of creation to war against those whom God created.

And I want you to notice very carefully the next move. One of the reasons Psalm 137 is rarely read in its entirety is because it spotlights the insanity of the cycle of violence and the cycle of hatred. Look at verse 9: "Happy shall they be who take your little ones and dash them against the rocks." The people of faith have moved from the hatred of armed enemies—these soldiers who captured the king; those soldiers who slaughtered his sons, put his eyes out; the soldiers who sacked the city, burned their town, burned their temple, and burned their towers—they moved from the hatred for armed enemies to the hatred of unarmed innocents. The babies. The babies. "Blessed are they who dash your babies' brains against a rock." And that, my beloved, is a dangerous place to be. Yet that is where the people of faith were in 551 B.C. And that is where far too many people of faith are in 2001 A.D. We have moved from the hatred of armed enemies to the hatred of unarmed innocents. We want revenge. We want paybacks, and we don't care who gets hurt in the process.

Now, I asked the Lord, what should our response be in light of such an unthinkable act? But, before I share with you what the Lord showed me, I want to give you one of my little Faith Footnotes. Visitors, I often give Faith Footnotes so that our members don't lose sight of the big picture.

Let me give you a little Faith Footnote. Turn to your neighbor and say Faith Footnote. I heard Ambassador Peck on an interview yesterday. Did anybody else see him or hear him? He was on Fox News. This is a white man and he was upsetting the Fox News commentators to no end. He pointed out that what Malcolm X said when he got silenced by Elijah Mohammed was in fact true, "America's chickens are coming home to roost."

We took this country by terror, away from the Sioux, the Apache, the Comanche, and the Navaho. Terrorism. We took Africans from their country to build our way of ease and kept them enslaved and living in fear. Terrorism. We bombed Grenada, killed innocent civilians, babies, non-military personnel. We bombed the black civilian community of Panama with stealth bombers, and killed unarmed teenagers and toddlers, pregnant mothers, and hard-working fathers. We bombed Khadafi's home and killed his child. "Blessed are they who bash your children's heads against the rock." We bombed Iraq, we killed unarmed civilians trying to make a living. We bombed a plant in Sudan as payback for an attack on our embassy, killed hundreds of hard-working people, mothers and fathers who left home to go out that day, not knowing they'd never get back. We bombed Hiroshima. We bombed Nagasaki—and we "nuked" far more than the thousands who died in New York and the Pentagon, and we never batted an eye. Kids playing in the playground, mothers picking up children after school—civilians not soldiers—people just trying to make it day by day. We have supported state terrorism against the Palestinians and black South Africans, and now we are indignant because the stuff we have done overseas is now brought right back into our own front yards. "America's chickens are coming home to roost."

Violence begets violence. Hatred begets hatred, and terrorism begets terrorism. A white ambassador said that y'all—not a black minister, not a reverend who preaches about racism—an ambassador whose eyes are wide open and who's trying to get us to wake up and move away from this dangerous precipice upon which we are now poised. The ambassador said the people overseas are wounded but don't have the military capability we do. We have superior military might, but they have individuals who are willing to die to take thousands with them, and we need to come to grips with that.

Let me stop my Faith Footnote right there, and ask you to think about that over the next few weeks if God grants us that many days. Now, come on back to my question to the Lord, "What should our response be right now in light of such an unthinkable act?" I asked the Lord that question: "What should our response be?"

I saw pictures of the incredible. People jumping from 110 floors. People jumping from the roof because the stairwells and elevators above the eighty-ninth floor were gone. Black people jumping to a certain death. People holding hands jumping. People on fire jumping, and I asked the Lord, "What should our response be?" I read what the people of faith felt in 551 B.C., but this is a different time; this is a different enemy; this is a different world; this is a different terror. This is a different reality. What should our response be?

The Lord showed me three things. Let me share them with you quickly, and I'm going to leave you alone to think about the Faith Footnote. Number one, the Lord showed me that this is a time for self-examination. As I sat nine hundred miles away from my family and my community of faith, two months after my own father's death, God showed me that this is a time for me to examine my relationship with God, my own relationship with God, my personal relationship with God. I submit to you it is the same for you. Folks flocked to the church where I was in New Jersey last week. You know that foxhole religion syndrome kicked in. That little red box you see that says: "Pull in case of emergency." It showed up full force. Folks who ain't thought about church in years were in church last week. I heard that mid-week prayer services all over this country, which are poorly attended fifty-one weeks a year, were jam-packed all over the nation.

But the Lord said, "This ain't the time for you to be examining other folks' relationships; this is the time of self-examination." The Lord said to me, "How is our relationship doing, Jeremiah? How often do you talk to me personally? How often do you let me talk to you privately? How much time do you spend trying to get right with me, or do you spend all your time trying to get other folk right?" This is a time for me to examine my own relationship with God. Is it real or is it fake? Is it forever or is it for show? Is it something that you do for the sake of the public, or is it something that you do for the sake of eternity? This is a time to examine my own and a time for you examine your own relationship with God. Self-examination. Then, this is a time—in light of the unbelievable tragedies—this is a time to examine my relationship with my family. Self-examination.

As soon as the first plane hit the World Trade Center, I called home, and I called my mother. Ramah was taking Jamila to the school bus, my mother's phone was busy, and the thought hit me, "Suppose you could never talk to her again? Suppose you never see Jamila, Janet, Jerry, Stevie, Jazzy, Jay, Ramah ever again?" What is the quality of the relationship between you and your family? The soul station in New York kept playing Stevie Wonder's song, "These Three Words." When is the last time you took the time to say to your family, "Honey, I love you"? And then that family thought led me to my extended family and my church family. We fight, we disagree, we fall out, we have diametrically opposed views on some critical issues, but I still love you. When is the last time you said that to your church family, when your daddy died? Well, that was two months ago. Reverend, you need to say that every chance you get. So let me just say that to you now. I love y'all. I love you. I love you. Listen. Listen. Don't clap. Turn to the person sitting next to you worshiping next to you and say it while you have the chance. Say, "I love you." Listen. Listen. This past week was a grim reminder of the fact that I might not have the chance to say that next week. So say it now: "I love you."

I had two deacons, two deacons: when they realized I could not fly home, two deacons got in a car and drove twelve straight hours, put my bags in the trunk, put me in the back seat, turned right around, and drove back twelve hours because they loved me. I want them to know, I love you. I love you. I love you. I thank God for you. Turn back and tell your neighbor one more time, "I love you." This is what a church family is, the beloved community, a community of love. Fights? Yes. Disagreements? Yes. Falling outs? Yes. Different viewpoints? Yes. Doctrinal disputes? Yes. But love that is of God and given by God who loved us so much that while we were yet sinners, God gave God's son rather than give up on us. This is the time of self-examination, a time to examine our personal relationships with God, a time to examine our personal relationships with our family, and a time to examine our personal relationships with our extended family, the family of God.

Then the Lord showed me this is not only a time for self-examination. This is also a time for social transformation. This is going to be the hardest step we have to take. But now is the time for social transformation. We have got to change the way we have been doing things. We have got to change the way we have been doing things as a society. Social transformation. We have got to change the way we have been doing things as a country. Social transformation. We have got to change the way we have been doing things as an arrogant, racist, military superpower. Social transformation. We just can't keep messing over people and thinking that, "Can't nobody do nothing about it." They have shown us that they can and that they will.

And let me suggest to you that rather than figure out who we gonna declare war on, maybe we need to declare war on racism. Maybe we need to declare war on injustice. Maybe we need to declare war on greed. Those same lawmakers you saw gathered at the capital praying are the same lawmakers who just passed a $1.3 trillion gift for the rich. Maybe we need to rethink the way we do politics and declare war on greed. Maybe we need to declare war on AIDS. In five minutes Congress found $40 billion to rebuild New York and for the families of those who died suddenly. Do you think we could find the money to make medicine available for people who are dying a slow death? We need to declare war on the health-care system that leaves the nation's poor with no health coverage. Maybe we need to declare war on the mishandled educational system and provide quality education for everybody, all citizens based on their ability to learn, not their ability to pay. This is a time for social transformation. We can't go back to doing business as usual and treating the rest of the world like we have been treating them. This is the time for self-examination. This is the time for social transformation.

But then ultimately I looked around and saw that God had given me another chance to try to be the man who God wants me to be, another chance to try to be the person that God meant for me to be. Another chance to try to be the parent that God knows I should be. Another chance to try to make a positive difference in a world full of hate. Another chance to teach somebody the difference between our God's awesomeness and our nation's arrogance. When I looked around and saw that for whatever the reason God had let me see another day, I realized that the Lord was showing me that this is not only a time for self-examination, this is not only a time for social transformation, but this is also a time for spiritual adoration. In other words, this is a time to say, "Thank you, Lord." This is the day that the Lord has made. I will rejoice and be glad in it. I may not have tomorrow, so I'm going to take this time on this day to say, "Thank you, Lord, thank you for my life." You didn't have to let me live. Thank you for my blessings. I could have been on one of those airplanes. I could have been in downtown New York or a few blocks from the Pentagon, but for whatever the reason you let me be here. So while I am here I'm going to take the opportunity to adore you, and to say, "Thank you, Lord." Thank you for the lives of those who were lost. Thank you for the way in which they touched our lives and the way in which they blessed other lives. Thank you, Lord. Thank you for the love we have experienced, and thank you, Lord, for the gift of our lives, because when I look around I realize that my life itself is a gift that God has given me, and so I say thank you. Thank you, Lord. While I have another chance, thank you. Just say it, thank you, Lord, for my friends and my family. Thank you, Lord, for this opportunity. Thank you for another chance to say thank you. If you mean that from your heart, throw your head back and adore him this morning. Say thank you, Lord. Thank you, Lord, for another chance. Another chance to say thank you. It's time for spiritual adoration.

Persevere
in Times
Like These

Manage Your Fear

Calvin O. Butts III

September 16, 2001

O my Comforter in sorrow, my heart is faint within me. Listen to the cry of my
people from a land far away: "Is the LORD not in Zion? Is her king no longer
there?" "Why have they provoked me to anger with their images, with their
worthless foreign idols?" "The harvest is past, the summer has ended, and we
are not saved." Since my people are crushed, I am crushed; I mourn, and horror
grips me. Is there no balm in Gilead? Is there no physician there? Why then is
there no healing for the wound of my people?   —Jeremiah 8:18-22, NIV

The United States of America has seen tragedy and I suspect, my
beloved sisters and brothers, that what makes this so different is simply its
enormity. But many of us can remember great tragedy in our nation, can't
we? Every so often the question is asked, Where were you when JFK was assassinated? We now feel grief and we feel horror and we feel sadness, but we
did then too, didn't we? It was almost for some of us like someone reached
into our bodies and snatched out our hearts. And we gasped when we heard
the news that someone had killed the president. Some of us are troubled as
we learn more and more about the horror at the World Trade Center especially, but let us not forget those who lost their lives in the Pentagon.

We are continually reminded now that the grieving process may not
be complete because the tremendous heat and the crushing pressure of the

descending frame of the World Trade towers and some of the surrounding buildings literally crushed beyond recognition or disintegrated the bodies of our beloved ones. For many of us there will be no bodies. And that's going to be difficult for some of us to get through because there will be no one to identify at the morgue. No coffin to pass by and take one parting glance. No one to mourn over, nothing to place in the ground. There will be no completion for some of the grieving proces, and we think, how terrible.

Oh, but beloved, we've been through these tragedies before. There was a TWA flight that fell from the skies—we don't really yet know the reason why—somewhere off the coast of Long Island. And don't you remember that many of those bodies were never found? The people could not complete their grieving process; still they go to the waters and cast flowers in memory of those who had passed away. It was not complete! America, we have seen these tragedies before. And I think the only thing that makes this any different is the enormity of it.

Where were you during the missile crisis? Remember the Cuban missile crisis? "They're going to bomb the United States!" they said. I remember as junior high school students we were forced into the cafeteria underground. We all remember the air raid shelters. Sometimes when we face these tragedies, we develop amnesia. We forget that many of us have been through this before, and we asked some of the same questions. Can't they protect the president now? Weren't there three others who were killed before Kennedy? Didn't they put into place certain precautions? How could this happen again? The day that will live in infamy—December 7, 1941—didn't we get some signals? Weren't there some omens? Where was the intelligence? Didn't they know that the Japanese were planning this? Where was America's security? Those questions sound familiar, don't they? We have heard and seen this before, and I think even though Pearl Harbor was enormous, it pales in the face of what has taken place here recently.

And so therefore, my beloved sisters and brothers, don't you look at this as if it's the end of the world. America, we've been through this before and guess what? We've come through it. You were here, some of you, in 1941, and you're here today. I was here when they assassinated the president and I thank God that I'm standing today. I remember the Cuban missile crisis, and I remember when that plane fell and I thought that the world might be coming to an end, that madness had engulfed our nation, that tragedy was the only thing that we would see. But, oh, thanks be to God, we came through it and we will come through it again.

Stand up, America. Oh, what a strange sound that is. We sound so unified. We sound so together. We're all flying the flag now. Oh, beloved, but now we realize, more than ever, how great it is to live in America. Never before in some of our lifetimes has tragedy visited our shores. But, thanks be to God that we have a country, that even though we've come face to face with terror, we are still able to pull together and thank God for beautiful skies and amber waves of grain. Thank God for our liberties that we enjoy. Thank God for our Constitution and the resolve of all Americans to pull together for the sake of our nation. I met with the governor and the mayor. Oh, Lord, have mercy, what tragedy will make us do! Black men and white men and Christians and Jews and Muslims are joining together with every other faith, plowing through the rubble on search-and-rescue missions. What counts now is not our differences.

What counts now is that we are all one in the greatest country in all the world, the United States of America. We appreciate it. Oh, our defenses perhaps were down. We could have been more secure. But we thank God for the men and the women who are now looking out for us, and now you understand why you've got to have those F-16s ready to fly. Now you understand why you've got to have the radar in the sky. Now you understand why more and more they're gonna hold you up a little longer as you go through the metal detector. They're gonna look through your bag and some will perhaps ask the question, "Why, why, why? I got a plane to catch." But most of us will say, "Thank you, thank you, thank you for protecting our security and making sure that we are able to enjoy the liberty that our Constitution grants to us."

We've been through this before, America, and we'll get through it again. We're strong, we're smart, and I want to say something else. Why are you so cast down? Sometimes I wonder if anybody is listening to the sermons other than me. And I had to ask myself the questions over and over again: Have I as a minister prepared the congregation that's under my watch for such a time as this? Have my sermons planted some seeds that might now have grown roots and the tree of faith has grown up in you, so that when tragedy like this strikes you're ready? That the root is so deep that you're like a tree planted by the waters, and even though the tragedy comes, you shall not be moved? Have I quoted enough Scripture, have I shared with you enough of what God has given me so that in the midst of it all, you can stand like the people of God?

One member took me to task a little while ago because I preached a sermon about death. She said, "Oh, Reverend, you could have preached a sermon about something else other than death." And I understood her concern. But, my beloved sisters and brothers, I want you to know that death—and I'm not going to spend a lot of time on it—but death comes. Doesn't it? And the only difference between the individual death of a loved one who may be crossing the street and getting run down by a driver who is crazed with alcohol, the death of a loved one who may be swimming in water off the coast of Florida and be gobbled up by a shark, the only difference between the death of a loved one who's suffering under the terrible scourge of AIDS or cancer and [the death of a loved one in] this tragedy is the enormity of it all.

It's not so much that we don't understand that people will die and we don't know how and we don't know when and we don't know where. It's just that all of this happened at one time, so big, so brazen, that we are all stunned and shocked by it. But think of the sister or brother who's here today or who's out there somewhere, who is going through his or her own pain because not only is there the enormity of the tragedy that was visited upon us, but also there is in his or her life the individual death of a mother or a father or a sister or a brother. You don't know when death is coming. Every time you step on a plane and you sit back and fasten your seatbelt—off you go into the wild blue yonder. But you don't know whether or not weather conditions or something beyond the pilot's control will snatch the plane from the sky. You don't know whether when you step out of your home one nice summer evening, some crazed maniac may hit you in the head for just a few dollars in your pocketbook. So death does not shock us, does it, beloved? It's just the enormity of this. But we all know that death is a-coming.

Then what are you worried about? "I am the Resurrection and the Life," sayeth the Lord. "He that believeth in me, though he were dead yet shall he live. And whosoever liveth and believeth in me shall never die." I serve a risen Savior! And even though death may come, I know in whom I believe, and he's got all power in his hand! God raised him from the dead and because he lives, I too shall live.

I mourn my brothers and sisters whose lives have been snatched by this tragedy, but my faith is in God through Christ and I know that one day, if I hold on and if I keep the faith, even if my friend has been snatched from me, I'll walk the streets of gold with my beloved. I'll see my friends again. I don't live as someone who has no hope. We'll get through it, America, because we've got a God somewhere who sits high and looks low. I trust in God. Wherever I may be upon the land or on the stormy sea, though billows roll, he keeps my soul. Oh, my heavenly Father, yes, he watches over me. We're gonna be all right, beloved. Because there's a God somewhere and that God is watching over us. That God is anointing those hands that are digging through the rubble. That God is anointing those men and women who are standing on corners directing traffic. That God is working with that man or woman who is trying to comfort some mother who is in crisis or some child who has been left an orphan. Our God has not forgotten us.

And, don't you ever say that this was the will of God! God does not will tragedy. God does not will death and destruction. God is not a monster! Our God is not a God of hate. Our God is not a God of mean-spiritedness. Our God is a God of love and peace and reconciliation. Don't you say that God is behind this. The will of God is not seen in tragedy. The will of God is seen in us. Oh, we are free and God permits evil, to allow our freedom to have full expression. But remember, God's will is in what you will do. God's will is in what you will say. So don't let God down. God is depending on us. God uses us and if the world is to know the love of God, it will know it through us, through those hands in the rubble. Thank God for those firefighters, police officers, and rescue workers.

We had an ecumenical prayer service. And one of the clergy persons said that when the buildings exploded and it was evident that there was going to be mass destruction, he watched as people ran out of the World Trade Center and the surrounding buildings. He said he could see them streaming out, running as fast as they could, eyes filled with fear but running. No computers, no pocketbooks, no books, no things, just running, dropping things on the way, he said. But then he witnessed an interesting thing. As the people were trying to keep a few steps ahead of the clouds of smoke and dust, he saw the fire personnel running *into* the building. Can you fathom that? People were running in fear away, but the firefighters were running *into* the building! Oh, beloved, don't let this terror make you afraid to do that which is right.

If those firefighters had not learned to manage their fear, there would be hundreds and, yea, even thousands more who would be dead. But because they were able—not to overcome, not to defeat, but to *manage* their fear—they were able to save countless numbers of people. Don't let fear paralyze you. Fear is natural. I'm scared now. I know that many of you are and I won't be foolish enough to stand here and tell you not to be afraid. Because there's a certain element of fear that lives in all of us. But beloved, manage your fear so that fear does not paralyze you.

Let me tell you what I mean. Some of you are saying now that you will never fly again. "I'm not gonna get on a plane ever again." Some of you have canceled trips and vacations and business journeys because you are afraid. Some of you will not ride the subways anymore. I've heard these expressions abound. Some of you are afraid to go across the Tri-Boro or the George Washington or the Throgs Neck Bridge or through the Holland, Lincoln, or Midtown Tunnel. Fear has paralyzed you! And beloved, if fear has paralyzed you, the terrorists have won. Yes, that's what the devil uses— fear. It keeps you from doing what you need to do. It keeps you from living life to its fullest. Remember those firefighters. They managed their fear. They moved because it was right, because love for humanity compelled them to put their fear behind them and to press on for the saving of life. So don't you let fear tie you up. You manage that fear. Get on that plane, because remember, you don't know when the time or the hour will come. It may not be on a plane. Don't let fear paralyze you! Get in that automobile, drive on across that bridge. Show the terrorists that they have not won! Show them that God is still on the throne of your heart. Show them! Fear is what they want. If they can strike fear in the hearts of the American people, they have won. If they can make us paralyzed by their terror, they have won. Don't you let fear stop you. Don't you know that there's a God above? Don't you know that there is someone who holds the whole world in their hands?

I'm talking to a predominantly African America congregation. Don't tell us about terror! We know terror. Oh, yes, we know terror. And don't allow people to go off on some tangent about Islamic terrorism or militant terrorism from Islam. Oh, religion is not the cause of this! Let me tell you about the terror we know. We know the terror that was called the Christian Knights of the Ku Klux Klan. No, we did not have World Trade Towers. We did not have a multi-trillion-dollar financial district. All we had was our homes and our churches. But the terror used to ride by night. They would rape our women, lynch our men, kill our children, burn our churches. We know terror! And the terror did not come with a star and a crescent. The terror was a burning cross on our front lawn. Oh, but during the civil rights struggle, when terror would come, we'd join our voices in song and sing: "We are not afraid today, deep in our hearts we do believe that we are not afraid today."

Don't let fear paralyze you. And remember, perfect love casts out all fear. Remember that uncle when that shark attacked that little boy? They said the uncle leaped on the shark and beat the shark; he hit it in its eye and made the shark let the little boy go. How many of you, if your children were attacked, wouldn't think about your own life? That love that you have for your child would put fear in the background. Don't be afraid.

And I'm all for building a memorial. Build a memorial. Build it in granite. Build it in platinum. Etch the names of those who lost their lives trying to save others. Build a memorial; light a candle that will burn eternally in their memory. But, I tell you, the greatest memorial that you can give to those firefighters is the memorial that you will not be afraid. Just as they weren't afraid to risk their lives, you've got to have the courage to live. *Live,* I tell you. Go on to work. *Live.* Raise your children. *Live.* And tell the devil that he does not have the victory. God has the victory!

We're filled with pain. You can't help but to feel pain in the face of this tragedy. And what is pain? Pain tells you that something is wrong in the body. Do you hear what I'm saying? It tells you that something has gone awry, that there is a problem somewhere. Now some pain you can just brush aside. "Oh, I got a little toothache but that's all right. I'm gonna go into work. I'll get it taken care of next week." Some pain you can just shrug off. "I got a little arthritis but that's all right. Let me kick my leg two times and get my third leg and I'll make it on down to the church," huh? Some pain you can just shrug off. "I got a little stomach trouble but get me some Pepto Bismol and I'll be all right."

But sometimes, pain is so great that it makes you double up. Have you ever had that kind of pain that makes your body tie up in knots? Sometimes pain is so great it makes you cry out in anguish: "Oh, Lord, what has got ahold of me?" And beloved, I'm telling you there's something wrong in the body of America. And the pain that we feel came as a result of the tragedy, and on that day the pain was so great that somebody had to call 911. It was an emergency, I tell you! There's something awry in our spirit. There's something wrong with us. You can't keep going without getting a wake-up call sometimes. And that wake-up call is telling us that if we're going to be an example to the world, we've got to learn first to start with ourselves. You can't point a finger at some other country or some other person, until we have first learned to love each other right here in America. If I can quote Rodney King, "We all got to learn how to get along."

There's too much hate between blacks and whites. Too much hate between Christians and Jews. Too much hate right here in America between those who are different. There's pain, I tell you! And let me tell you, when you got emotional pain, you try to cover it up with anger. Yeah, you know. You ever had your heart broken? You ever been jilted by a lover? It causes you pain, but you try to mask it with anger. How you doing today? Leave me alone. Why don't you come on over? I don't want to go anywhere today. Don't you run into people like that? They seem to be angry all the time. That's because they're hurting deep down inside. And sometimes anger covers up your pain. So when you see people marching through neighborhoods that are not their own, chanting "U-S-A," it's because they've got pain and they're using the anger to cover up that pain. When you see people attacking folk who may speak another language or who may look like they come from another country, it's because of pain and the anger is to strike out against the pain.

Oh, beloved, but I'm telling you, there is a balm in Gilead. That balm in Gilead is named Jesus, and those of us who have seen the terror of the night riders know that we can find comfort in his name. Jesus is our rock in a weary land. Our Jesus is our shelter in a time of storm. Our Jesus is our bridge over troubled waters, and when we're going through this kind of pain, rather than get angry, that balm in Gilead says, "Vengeance is mine, I will repay, sayeth the Lord." That balm in Gilead says you can't conquer this all by yourself because your fight is not against flesh and blood but against principalities and powers. That balm in Gilead soothes a sin-sick soul and helps you to get control of your anger and begin to seek out something that will ease your pain. When we come to this [Communion] table today, beloved, here's our balm in Gilead. Here's our physician; we call him affectionately Dr. Jesus. He has a way of calming our nerves and soothing our fears. This Jesus has a way of making a way out of no way. He can calm the troubling waters. He can stop the evil winds from blowing. And when we come to the table, I'm gonna say something that may sound like an anathema to some. But beloved, everybody is welcome at this table. I don't care if you're Muslim or Jewish. You're welcome at this table. Because our Lord was not crucified for some. Our Lord was not raised up from the dead for some. But our Lord was crucified and raised for all, and everybody has a right to this balm in Gilead.

And so today, my beloved sisters and brothers, I tell you don't worry about a thing. We've been this way before and we'll come through it. Don't worry about the enormity of the death. Death is terrible at any number. Don't worry about fear. Overcome your fear. Manage your fear, and remember to keep on living your life. We've seen terror. We've seen the lightning flashing and heard the thunder roll, but God has been with us. And even though you feel pain, remember that there is a balm in Gilead. You know the summer's over, the harvest is complete, and some of us are still not saved.

I was upstairs earlier today. Rev. Dease was up stairs. She was just jumping to the song, "Oh, I'm glad to be in the service, glad to be in the service, glad to be in the service, one more time." She was by herself, you know. Nobody else there but she was just jumping and dancing. Happy, clapping her hands. You know why? Because Rev. Dease knows that she's safe in the arms of Jesus. She knows there's no sense in us crying too long, that life has to go on. She's rooted and anchored in God. And beloved, even though Colin Powell and the president have got to assemble their planes and their tanks and their bombs, remember that the old prophet said: "Not by power, not by might but by my Spirit, sayeth the Lord." And also remember this, that as you look down now for those World Trade Towers and you don't see them, don't you be discouraged. Just remember that little song that we sing and you'll realize that all of these things will soon pass away. Oh, beloved, I want you to "build your hopes on things eternal and hold to God's unchanging hand." And with God's hand in our hand we will overcome. We will move forward; we will claim the victory. America will be strong. We will rebuild, and we will heal the pain in our hearts. There is a balm in Gilead. There is a physician, Jesus Christ our Lord. Amen. God bless you.

No Test, No Testimony

Jesse Louis Jackson Sr.
SEPTEMBER 16, 2001

We thank and praise God for the privilege to be here today. We're not here because we're lucky. We're here because we're blessed. We're not here because we're so smart, because we have a strong wall to protect us. There are no walls of protection. The nation is laid bare. And so we come to God, for God is our refuge. Wall Street is not our refuge. The Pentagon is not our refuge. God is our refuge: an ever-present help in a time of trouble.

This day I want us to have an experience together. We're still in a state of trauma. And pain besets us. When the sun is eclipsed at high noon, there's radical disorientation. Chickens flap their wings and give birth prematurely. Dogs bark. Cats scratch. People pull to the side of the road. The clock stops. It's trauma. And in our period of trauma, we must not let trauma be our voice and our guide. We must do something now. We couldn't stop the planes from hitting the buildings. But we want to do something. We reach out to family and friends. All of us are touched. We want to do something.

I want the churches to become trauma centers, because members have questions, and they need reasonable, accessible answers. And I want our psychologists and psychiatrists to connect with our ministers and set up trauma lines for counseling. I want our teachers and psychiatrists to connect, because our children know that we've seen CNN wars; we've seen Nintendo wars. This is not ketchup. This is real blood. And our children feel the trauma. I want the disc jockeys, who talk to so many people, to be in communication with the psychiatrists and ministers that we might have some consistent word of hope. And so, as a part of this experience today, some can do counseling and some can give blood. People need blood in Washington. They need blood in New York. They need blood for future attacks; the war is not over.

Sign up today to give blood to the Red Cross. Thank God you have some blood to give. We come because it's the right thing to do. And we don't know whether our blood will go to an Arab or a Jew or a black or a white or a gay or a straight. That suggests one blood. And if you need some blood, you're not gonna ask if it's black or straight or gay or Jewish or Arab. It suggests one blood. And so one blood. One people. There is no ghetto, barrio, suburban hiding place when the hounds of hell bomb. On this past Tuesday the janitors, the maids, the managers, the bosses, those wearing uniforms and those wearing striped suits, lions and lambs, had to lie together when the storms of life did rage. And so we're one in the spirit. We're one in the blood. We're one in the challenge.

I want you to get your Bibles and turn to the Book of Job. The Book of Job, the third chapter and the twenty-fifth verse: "For the thing which I greatly feared is come upon me, and that which I was afraid of is come unto me" (KJV). Then, in Job the thirteenth chapter and the fifteenth verse, "Though he slay me, yet will I trust in him: but I will maintain mine own ways before him" (KJV). And Luke the eighth chapter and the twenty-second verse through the twenty-fifth:

> Now it came to pass on a certain day, that he went into a ship with his disciples: and he said unto them, "Let us go over unto the other side of the lake." And they launched forth. But as they sailed he fell asleep: and there came down a storm of wind on the lake; and they were filled with water, and they were in jeopardy. And they came to him, and awoke him saying "Master, Master, we perish." Then he arose, and rebuked the wind and the raging of the water: and they ceased, and there was a calm. And he said unto them, "Where is your faith?" And they being afraid wondered, saying one to another,

"What manner of man is this! for he commandeth even the winds and water, and they obey him." (KJV)

I want to talk from the subject "No test, no testimony." In many ways, it's a difficult sermon to convey, because all of our hearts are so heavy, and so anxiety ridden. I feel deeply the pain of that myself. As I walked through the rubble of the Pentagon last night and talked with the relatives of lost ones, it's different than television. It's so real. I was shocked and horrified by the events of this week.

On Tuesday morning there was a story sent to us at prime time, and there was no time for programming interruption. On live television, a hijacking suicide bombing took place. But not one, not two, not three, but four. Most hijackings end at airports, but this time that was not the destination. The outcome was totally unpredictable and beyond our imagination.

I began to go over my Middle East experiences, trying to connect what happened and how shall we respond. There are some things different about the cultures. We read left to right, they read right to left. We're driven by instant newscasts. They're driven by a different timetable of history. I thought about my trips to Syria to help bring Lieutenant Robert Goodman back home. About going to Baghdad, Iraq talking to Saddam Hussein, and securing the release of six hundred women. About going to Kuwait to try to save a Palestinian woman trapped in the rubble; about going to Libya and going to Yugoslavia and to Bosnia Herzegovina. I thought about the differences in headlines during these trips. If a Chicago Bear runs a touchdown in Chicago and they win a game, it's a big headline in Chicago. It's in a small column in Washington. The Washington Redskins run a touch down and win a game in Washington, it's a small column in Chicago. And so according to where you are determines the size of headlines. In each instance they focused on me as a person, as a personality. Jesse meeting with another tyrant. I met with the tyrant because the tyrant had the keys to the jails that were holding our people. If my friends were in hell, and the only way I could get them out was to go to the devil to get them, I'd go to the devil and give him an air-conditioner or some gift. I'd go down there, too.

But what was missed in each news report—in Syria, in Iraq, for those cultures—was the tone set by the culture. Just as Billy Graham, Jerry Falwell, and Pat Robertson set the tone for this culture.

I reflected upon the president's meeting at Camp David this weekend, trying to earnestly determine a response to the crisis. I wondered if there were any Middle Easterners in the room, if there were any clerics in the room. If it is understanding that we seek and strategies that must be devised in this clash of cultures and values, what do we see?

Today we mourn, we weep. We mourn the loss of loved ones, we mourn the nation gripped in trauma. We mourn the injury to our national pride, this radical shift from overconfidence to uncertainty in the blinking of an eye. We mourn the wreckage of monuments, the Twin Towers symbolizing our money, the Pentagon symbolizing our might. Symbols of economic prosperity and military prowess. We have been stabbed in the heart. It all leaves us in trauma, in search of answers. Why now? Why the United States? Or why so many innocent people? Our sun was eclipsed at high noon. Our leaders seek to offer us assurance. But even they weep. The trauma has led to disorientation. Thus, we see through a glass darkly. We know in part. We learn not merely to think, but lean not to our own understanding but on thee. We are sustained by God's Word, not our works, and that will get us through. But only by grace and mercy. The night is long. Is it evening time or morning time? Is it twilight moving toward midnight? Or is it dawn? The night is long, the pain is deep. But God promised that, the "weeping may endureth for a night, joy will come in the morning." But the night is still upon us, and we long for the morning. In our trauma and in our distress, we say traumatized things and may engage in traumatized acts. But the Lord has brought us thus far and lifted us too high to come down now.

So I turn to Job. The man who said, "If a man dies (he asked a question) shall he live again?" Then he said: "But all of my appointed days, I will wait until my change comes." Job, like us, had known great prosperity. Job had done many great works. Though unlike Job, we are not always perfect and upright, and yet we've been a beacon of light and hope for many. Like Job, we question, why us? We speak of Job's patience. Job was not patient. Job was known more for his suffering and not surrendering than for his patience. Job did not curse God, but he cursed everybody else. He cursed the day he was born. Job cursed September 11. He cursed the night his mother conceived him in her womb. He cursed his seed, he cursed his birth. He prayed that he had been still-born. He wished to have been in darkness and death before he knew the joys of life. This guy Job.

We've heard lots of pained, angry talk since Tuesday. [Jerry] Falwell, the Reverend in his gullible, cultural, instinctual way, said it was because of gays and abortions. Traumatized talk. Some congressman said, "Revive the policy to assassinate other leaders." Traumatized people. Some generals said, "Shoot in the dark for the phantom terrorist. Disregard collateral damage and killing of innocent people." Traumatized talk. Just hit somewhere, hit somebody. Relieve us of our anger. We feel the crosswinds of being the most powerful nation, the most vulnerable, maybe now the most helpless. But helplessness must not deteriorate into hopelessness. In a time like this, we who have known God in victory, we who have known God in prosperity, we who have known God as the lone superpower, we who have known wind blowing behind our backs pushing us forward—we must not have a faith-deficit disorder in a time of crisis.

Job says—watch this—"For the thing which I feared the most has come upon me." Even in our bragging prosperity, we really fear we might lose it. When we show up bragging about our genius, we know it is just one step between us and failure. With all of our success, we really know deep down that we are just one step from failure in this system. And since it is not totally of us, there's always a fear we can't do it.

And so Job says, "I have money, I have land, I have family, I have cattle, I have a big name, I'm a famous person. All the headlines about me are good. After all I own the only newspaper in town and I read my own clippings and I'm perfect unto myself. I'm upright and no one can talk back because I hired most of the people in town. I've surrounded myself with my own newspaper and my own employees, and I am the philanthropist for the local school. I fund most of the politicians, and so I'm surrounded by prosperity and the great reputation for being a genius. But I feared just beneath all of that, that some time, some way, it might come to an end."

And so Job says after he lost his wife and children and faith, "That which I feared the most." That telephone call: you just lost your favorite son in college. That telephone call: you just lost a daughter or a loved one. They called. Trade buildings are falling down. They've hit the Pentagon; they pierced our shields. Job said, "That which I feared the most has come upon me."

This is a different kind of war. It's a war on our own soil, not on our terms. All of our *Saturday Evening Post* pictures, our *Newsweek* and *Time* magazine pictures, our *Washington Post*, *New York Times* pictures are at the seashore waving at the ship. "Go conquer, and we'll wait for you." They are at some airforce base—kiss good-bye—I'll be back and I know I'll be back because we have the best of ships. We have the best of planes, and you've seen these CNN Nintendo wars, and we win them and we will be back. And yet now it's a war, not over yonder but down the street. It's always been veterans of foreign wars. Now it will be veterans of domestic wars.

We always feared that temporary allies would turn on us and become long-term enemies. We helped to finance bin Laden. We supplied him weapons, and now the attack dog has bitten the master. We feared this. We feared the loss of freedom and openness to police-state security. We feared the suspension of civil liberties. We feared the loss of confidence in our defense system from real threats. We paid big money. We built exotic weapons. We controlled the air, the land, the sea, and yet the tall symbols of our money and our might today are smoking ruins.

Job said, "What I feared the most has come upon me." Americans turning on Americans. Scapegoating Muslim Americans. Scapegoating Arab Muslims. It was not right for Hitler to scapegoat the Jews in Germany. It was not right for us to scapegoat the Japanese Americans and put them in camps. In Oklahoma City, when the bombing took place, the experts got on TV and they began to draw a picture. They began to draw these imaginary pictures, smart men who make smart bombs because they were in trouble. They said it looked Middle Eastern, Arab-like. It wasn't Middle East or even Middle America. It was Tim McVeigh. These black kids are dangerous, better watch them. Three strikes and you're out. Mandatory sentencing. They wear their hair differently. They wear tattoos. They curse on records. Lock them up; then we'll be safe. So we locked them up, and then came Columbine. We locked them up, and then came Paducah, Kentucky, and Mississippi. And so scapegoating our neighbors is wrong and dangerous.

Remember: for every complex problem there's a simple answer and it's always wrong. Redemption and revival will not be found in bigotry. We have the suburban homes and the manicured lawns and a bedroom for each of our children, but they can't sleep. They're wetting the bed. They're having nightmares. The parents can't answer their questions. The ministers can't answer their questions. The disc jockeys can't answer their questions. The politicians can't answer their questions. We don't have immediate answers, but yet we must not in our trauma choose short-term pleasure that will lead to long-term pain.

What we feared the most was our adversaries. We've become embittered, alienated, hostile enemies. They were not born that way. What is the source of their unfathomable anger? Of their unfathomable bitterness?

Job said, "What I feared the most has come upon us." As we walked and prayed last night with victims' families and counseled them, I had begun to try to think the process through. My mind walked the roads of Damascus and Baghdad and Yugoslavia, as I tried to hear a word. First of all, y'all, we're fighting a global foe. If you're fighting a global foe, you must choose coalition over isolation. You must choose multilateral over unilateral. Not long ago we were saying to Europe about treaties and capital punishment and Star Wars, we'll go it alone. We were saying to the Middle East that we will not get involved to reconcile, signs that we will do diplomacy by ultimatum and not by negotiation. And we told South Africa, too, we said we are too busy. But now as we find a global foe, everybody matters.

There's a call for unity by the president and he's right to call for it. And we need global unity. There's a unity in pain; we all hurt. There's unity in passion, a unity in our fear of attacks, unity in humiliation and in national pride. But the issue is unity of vision, a vision of the source, nature, and location of the threat. The intelligence of the nature, source, and location of the threat will help determine our strategy and the nature of our task.

Today the foes are on our soil. No uniforms, high-tech, connected, American-trained. The world has changed since Tuesday, but has our view of the world changed since Tuesday? The president called for unity. We should join him. He says, Let's fight terrorism. Well, if we are going to fight it, define it. Define it universally, and apply it universally. We say we have nuclear definitions and we define nuclear threat and we address nuclear accountability because nuclear weapons have been a threat to us. Now terrorism is a threat. And so we must define it, and apply rules to stop it everywhere.

We were stabbed in the heart on Tuesday. I watched as much of the talk shows as I could. I heard a little from Capitol Hill, and I've heard the news commentators, and almost all of them assume there was a military collapse. Now they want a military solution. We still have the strongest military in the history of the world. Y'all follow me now. Our military policy is strong. It was our intelligence policy and our diplomatic policy and economic policy that must be addressed. You must look at military intelligence, diplomacy, and economics in the same basket. Will y'all follow me for a minute? If we knew where the enemy was, we would get the enemy. There have been several bits of good news this week. They were going to board a plane in New York again and we caught them. They were going to board a plane in L.A. and we caught them this week. They were going to board a plane in Chicago. They had false IDs. and false airline licenses. And we caught them. We caught them with intelligence.

I know with some of them we say, "Well, when we find them, we'll bomb them where they were trained, and we'll get them." But some of them were trained in Florida, which complicates our search. We will bomb them, but some of them were trained in Germany. Will we bomb Germany? Some in Afghanistan. This week we have been reasonably successful to stop additional attacks with precise intelligence, not indiscriminate bombing. So far this week, with precise intelligence, timely intelligence, we've been made more secure. We have superior weapons over our foes, but they have superior intelligence. They know where our weaknesses are. The enemy is in the camp; it's like a virus. Military policy, intelligence policy, diplomatic policy. Today our troops are building a circle around Afghanistan. But there is Iraq, that we have been bombing for ten years. And they don't think kindly of us. And there's Libya; there's the Sudan, where we blew up a medical manufacturing plant. I've gone to the Great 8 Nations Summit meetings where the industrial, powerful nations meet. And they leave on one accord and they take the big picture, the big eight. But you go to the nonaligned conference meeting where the majority of poor people in the world are and there's this angst toward our nation.

Somehow, where there is military readiness, there must also be diplomatic readiness and intelligence readiness and economic readiness. When I look at our allies, what contributes to their being allies? For our allies we provide for them trade, investment, infrastructure, universal exchanges, and military protection. Our allies, every one of them, have aid, trade infrastructure, transportation, investments, loan debt forgiveness, and defense. They are our allies. But our adversaries—we have the opposite program for them it seems. We need to have a plan. If they had a five-year plan to destroy us, we cannot have a one-weekend plan to stop it.

I love America, and I have traveled this world telling the story about our great country. I've heard the rattling, the pain, and the discomfort. Let's begin to journey out of the hole. This is not a shouting kind of a sermon. Will y'all bear with me a few minutes? How shall we deal with being on the ground? Job said, "What I feared the most is upon us." We have not known the canvas before. Not long ago Lennox Lewis was in a fight. And he was so convinced he was going to win, he did a movie rather than prepare for the fight. He was planning his next movie when the fight was held. And suddenly, around the corner, came a devastating left hook. He woke up at about the count of fifteen saying, "Are our children ready for school? It's time to go to work." Referee waving, he said, "Are the children ready for school? It's time to go to work." He was on the canvas. He was completely in shock. He was talking about children going to school and going to work, and the fight was over. He was traumatized.

Watch this. Ali got knocked down one night and about the count of five he started wobbling. And about seven, he grabbed one leg again. Grabbed the rope and around nine he stood up. So his trainer said, "Stop." Ali said, "No, I have got to keep going. I have got to keep—." They said, "Stop." He said, "I can buy time until it's over." He weaved, he bobbed until it was over and got to the corner, and they put the cold water in his face. And he began to be revived and he went on and he finally won the fight. Pained, but he won the fight. And so when the announcer said, "Ali, you were down, you could have just laid there. You were hurt." He said, "I was hurt." The announcer said, "But your trainer said stop." He said, "I know." "Why did you get up?" He said, "Because the ground is no place for a champion."

America, we may be down, but don't lie there. The ground is no place for a champion. You may have a hurting head, you may have a black eye. But don't wallow there. The ground is no place for a champion. "The thing I feared the most." The arrogance of my power, the idolatry of my might, my tower of money and might was pierced. I can't use my airports, I can't watch football. I can't watch baseball. I am in trauma. The thing I feared the most is upon me.

Watch this. The difference between the blues and the gospel is the blues feeds upon the blues. The blues speaks of going down twice and coming up once. But with the gospel you go down but you get up again. Say, "I fall down, but I get up again!"

Jesus had been out preaching—sunshine, blue sky, not a cloud in the sky. Jesus was fatigued, so he laid down, the Bible said, "in the hind part of the ship." The disciples—his bodyguards, his running partners—felt a sense of uppityness. After all, Jesus had walked among the crowd and they had been support agents. And sometimes those who are support agents think they're the man. And they got so carried away with themselves, they started running people away. A woman and her children wanted to see Jesus. "He busy." Jesus said, "No, you ain't me. You're an usher. I'm trying to preach folks into church; you're trying to run them out. Stop. Let the old folks wait. Let the little children come unto me." With all this power he maintained humility.

The disciples got carried away, so on this boat that day Jesus was sleeping, and a storm came suddenly. Storms don't need your permission to come. They don't have to forewarn you they're coming. And they don't come by race; they don't come by religion. You can be a Hindu or a Christian or a Jew or a Catholic. An airline pilot says when you get on the plane, "Put your seat belt on." Why? He says, "I think it's going to be a good ride. There are no clouds between Chicago and Washington, but in case there is some clear-air turbulence, have your seat belt on before the storm."

Some folks started talking to God on Tuesday afternoon. Some people who had never shown up at the cafeteria want to jump to the front of the line. "Hey God, looka here! How can you do this to me?" Some folks who were not under his commandments, who were not going to church, who were not tithers, have been the first in line. You ought really put your seat belt on before the plane takes off, because there may be clear-air turbulence and the storm might come suddenly.

And who do you turn to when fate deals you a dirty blow? You can't fight fate by cursing. Job found that out. You can't fight fate with your money. You can't hit fate with your fist. You can't cut fate with your knife. You can't shoot fate with your gun. You cannot bribe fate with your clothes. You can't impress fate with your body build. Fate is an awesome foe. You cannot fight fate with words. You fight fate with faith. Faith fights fate.

When the storms of life come suddenly, there are some storm rules. The first rule is when a storm comes, know that it is a storm. Don't think a storm is an April shower. Storms have more power than April showers. So if your house is built on sand, you can't take storms.

The second point is that when storms come, don't panic. Don't open your mouth and close your eyes, thinking you're going to drown! "If it hadn't been for you, I wouldn't have been in this ship. I shouldn't have been—I should have followed my first mind. I was doing pretty good before I met you. Ever since I been around you, ain't been nothing but trouble. That's why I ain't got no job because you got a job." You start getting irrational. You start turning on the Arab Americans. You start turning on the Jews. You start turning on the blacks. When the storm comes, don't panic and scapegoat. You cannot stop a storm by turning on your neighbor. When storms come, don't jump ship. You're too far from shore. You can't swim there. When storms come, build coalitions; reject isolation. You can't make it by yourself. If you're going to fight terrorism, you need some folk you've not spoken to in a long time. Pakistan, what's happening, buddy? When storms come you need coalition, you can't make it by yourself.

This is my last point. When the storms of life come, the first instinct is to panic. The disciples were selfish, and they panicked. But, at least down in their gut they knew who the anchor was. When the storms of life rage— and they rage sometimes—who do you turn to? The disciples called on the captain of the ship. When the storms of life rage, and buildings are falling and leaders are stumbling and crying, who do you turn to? What do you turn to? Turn to your faith and not to your fear. When the storms of life rage, get up off that ground. The ground is no place for a champion. I've got a power that you can't stop, that you can't see. It's called faith. The substance of things hoped for, the evidence of things unseen. "Faith of our fathers living still." I can't prove faith but I know, because I know, because I know, there's a power in my faith. It's dark, but the morning comes. Faith.

The Lord is our light and our salvation; whom shall we fear? We should not fear bombs; who shall be feared? Nobody. The Lord is our light. We get scared sometimes, but "Yea, though I walk through the valley of the shadow of death, I will fear no evil, for thou art with me. Thy rod and thy staff, they comfort me." Yes, I was up, and now I'm down. "Yet though you slay me,"—though buildings fall, though confusion abounds—"yet will I trust you." You've been too good to me. "Yet will I trust you." You've brought me from too far back. You've lifted me up when I was down. "Yet will I trust you." I will not give up on God now.

"If my people, who are called by my name, will humble themselves and pray and seek my face and then turn"—I said turn, I said turn—from their wicked ways, then God will forgive us for our sins, and then we will hear from heaven and then God will heal our land. Heal our land. Heal our land. Heal our land. God will. God will. God will heal our land. God will. God will. God will heal our land. . . .

Preaching While the World Is at War!

Carolyn Ann Knight

September 28, 2001

On December 14, 1941, one week after the attack on Pearl Harbor, the Reverend Harry Emerson Fosdick, senior pastor of the Riverside Church in New York City, preached a sermon entitled "The Church of Christ in a Warring World." In that sermon Dr. Fosdick acknowledged the harsh realities of the world at war and raised the question about the role the church should have in it. Dr. Fosdick said: "Our nation is at war, not as a matter of choice but of fact, and this situation confronts us saying, 'You, the Church of Christ, hating war, as you ought to, finding in it as you should, the denial of everything Christ stands for, what positively are you going to do for your generation now?'"[1] Fosdick admonished the church to be active participants in the struggle against the ravages of the evils of war. Fosdick challenged the church to be like the leaven that gives rise to bread, to help the nation rise out of the ashes of the conflict of war.

On Tuesday, September 11, 2001, the words of Harry Emerson Fosdick once again rang true. We are at war, not as a matter of choice but of fact. Preachers in America once again find themselves struggling with the role of the church in a nation at war. The bombing of the World Trade Center in New York City and the Pentagon building in Washington, D.C., as well as the aborted attempt of a third terrorist bombing, plunged the United

States into the type of domestic conflict that we have only seen on TV and read about in the newspapers. Until now, we have seen the ugly face of war and terrorism through the sanitized, pristine lenses of a nightly newscast. But on that fateful Tuesday, we became participants in this horrific drama.

On Monday many preachers in this nation were just thinking about what we would like to preach on Sunday. On Tuesday we all had our sermon subject, if not our Scripture for the sermon. Preachers who were in the middle of a sermon series were forced to put the series aside and focus on the situation that had changed the world forever. During the week I received many phone calls from colleagues, friends, and students wondering what they should preach or if a particular Scripture would be suitable for the occasion.

At first, I was startled by the question, "What should I preach?" My initial response to the question was to answer the way I believed the late Dr. Samuel DeWitt Proctor would answer: "There is always plenty of gospel to preach; open the Bible and pick a text!" Then it dawned on me that my friends and colleagues in the preaching ministry were facing a new reality. Just as the world had changed for all of us, preaching for them had changed as well. Few of us who preach in this day and age have had to face congregations that were frightened and fearful about their families, their finances, and their future. Many of us have never watched and wondered what would happen next. After all, we live in a day of casual Christianity, effortless religion, and spur-of-the-moment spirituality.

In addition to the concern for our congregations and cities, many of us struggled with our own emotions, questions, and fears. I am from New York and was offered my first full-time ministerial position at the Windows on the World restaurant, which was on top of the World Trade Center. So my emotions ran the full gamut from shock to deep sadness to anger to uncontrollable tears. But I also wondered about the shape of the sermon in light of this new reality we were facing. Like it or not, we are preachers and prophets in a world that is at war.

Part of the problem most preachers have with preaching is that there is always a Sunday morning on the horizon. No matter what happens anywhere in the world, there is always a Sunday coming and a sermon must be preached. Preachers are not afforded the luxury of having Sunday off.

Sunday is the day when preachers must go to work. Preachers must be prepared to go into the pulpit with a word from God regardless of the events that take place in their lives and in their world. This is what we have been called by God and the congregation to do. God calls us—and the congregation entrusts us—to go to the Scriptures week in and week out to faithfully interpret the Word of God on their behalf. Preachers and pastors now find themselves preaching to a congregation that has the threat of war right here in the United States before their eyes and in their minds. Now we are at war, and our preaching must comfort, challenge, and counsel.

Many are the needs of the members in our congregations that must be addressed by the preacher. Those of us who preach in the days ahead must address the needs of our congregations as they struggle with fears and concerns about the economy and their safety. Thousands of jobs have already been lost. The employment and economic futures of many in this nation are uncertain. There will be more layoffs. There will be funeral and memorial services. Then there is the concern that we must have for our children and young people. The preacher will need to speak in a therapeutic way to the concerns of young people, who may have nightmares about the events that affect their lives and about their fear of the future.

Beyond all these concerns, some members of our congregations will be going to fight in this global conflict. The preacher will need to preach sermons that encourage these people to be courageous in battle. Families of these brave soldiers will need to hear words of comfort and encouragement from the pulpit.

The President of the United States, in a speech to the nation delivered before the Congress, determined that this will be a long, drawn-out confrontation, fought in unconventional ways. President Bush said there will be some battles that we in this nation are aware of and others we will not be aware of. If this is the case, this war we are fighting will come up in our preaching again and again. Preachers and pastors will have to be extremely sensitive to the mood of their congregations. They will have to know when there are issues that need to be addressed and when the membership is in need of a sermon that doesn't even mention the word *war*. The preacher will need to develop sermons that strike a balance between the events in the world and the congregation's need for spiritual growth and nurture, independent of any war.

In the days, weeks, and months ahead, money will need to be raised and more blood will need to be donated. Our young men and women who are being deployed to foreign lands will welcome a word from home, even if that word is coming from a stranger. Pastors can encourage their members, especially the young ones, to write to these soldiers who are far away from home. As the news reaches that the battle is escalating, pastors will need to gather their members for prayer at a moment's notice. We will all have to struggle with our desire to criticize the military industrial complex in order to comfort those families directly affected by it. The preacher will need to be prepared to address these concerns as they unfold from day to day. Add to all of this the myriad of issues and congregational concerns that require the sermonic eye of the preacher.

On the day after that fateful Tuesday when I was able to settle my thoughts and think about my own preaching, I was drawn to the writings of Harry Emerson Fosdick, Paul Tillich, Martin Luther King Jr., Dietrich Bonhoeffer, and Reinhold Niebuhr. These preachers and theologians all faced the challenge of preaching in wartime. It was interesting to revisit their sermons and to know what they had to say to a world at war. I found in some of the sermons harsh criticisms of war under any circumstances and, in others, explanations as to why it was necessary to fight. In all of them, I found a clear confidence about the justice of God and the love of Jesus Christ.

These sermons made in their time—as ours must now—a strong declaration about the power of the pulpit and preaching in times like these. D. Elton Trueblood, a Quaker, said that "in times of crisis a strong and vital pulpit is essential to the hope and restoration of the nation." Harry Emerson Fosdick, in a volume of sermons preached in wartime entitled *A Great Time to Be Alive,* said that in times of war the pulpit must return the nation to a sense of calm and stability. I believe that this is a very important time for the African American pulpit to be the conscience of this nation. I believe that this will be a tremendous time for preachers and pastors to bring their congregations back to matters of utmost significance in the church and in this nation.

What, then, is the role of the pulpit when the world is at war? Well, the pulpit has the same mandate it has in time of peace—that is to preach the gospel of our Lord and Savior Jesus Christ. In times of peace and war, God demands that we "love mercy, do justly, and walk humbly with our God." We are to preach in such a way that those who listen to our sermons understand that God has made these claims upon our lives, so that we may be lovers and makers of peace.

I believe that out of this tragedy some great preaching will come. Preachers will be challenged in new ways to search the Scriptures and discover what God is saying to the church in a time like this. Those of us entering the pulpit in the days and weeks ahead will have to face listeners who all week long have been inundated by headlines and newspaper stories that report the uncertainty of the times. We must reassure them that God is in charge of our future as God is in charge of our today. Let us resolve that out of this tragedy and the uncertain future we face shall come some of the best preaching of the twenty-first century. I want to suggest that we who preach in this dark hour should not shrink from the daunting task before us. Rather we should face each Sunday morning with a renewed determination that God is always speaking in the midst of chaos, confusion, and conflict.

---

[1]Robert Moats Miller, *Harry Emerson Fosdick: Preacher, Pastor, Prophet* (New York: Oxford University Press, 1985).

It Is Time to Move Forward!

Vashti Murphy McKenzie

September 16, 2001

But Moses said to the people, "Do not be afraid, stand firm, and see the deliverance that the LORD will accomplish for you today; for the Egyptians whom you see today you shall never see again. The LORD will fight for you, and you have only to keep still."

Then the LORD said to Moses, "Why do you cry out to me? Tell the Israelites to go forward." —Exodus 14:13-15, NRSV

T his is a good time to take inventory. In the wake of September 11, 2001 we need to re-access our values, reestablish our priorities, and scrutinize our relationship with Jesus Christ.

It is amazing that at times such as these we are forced to take a long hard look at who we are, what we value, what we deem important. We are compelled to examine what or in whom we really believe.

The terrorist attack has shaken us in ways that no other event in history has done. We all remember where we were when the news came from Dallas, Texas, that President John F. Kennedy was assassinated. We remember what we were doing the day the news came from Tennessee that Martin Luther King Jr. was shot and killed on the balcony of the Lorraine Hotel. We remember vividly when we gazed with amazement at the gaping hole in the Federal Building in Oklahoma City. We remember how horrified we were watching high school students escape from Columbine High School in Colorado.

We were viewing a steady diet of tragedies and trials in our living rooms via a multiplicity of media. Child pornography, vulgarity, apartheid, ethnic cleansing, state-sponsored religious persecution, child slavery, torture, genocide, rampant racial profiling, political assassinations, race-based political asylum, and neo-nazism became apart of our daily ritual, like drinking morning coffee.

The atrocities of the world are no longer happening to other people. It is happening to us. What happened on Tuesday—three airplanes used as cruise missiles, destroying two symbols of financial power and tarnishing the symbol of American military might, and one missing its mark, crashing in a Pennsylvania field. Thousands are missing and presumed dead.

Nothing has touched us, moved us, hurt us, shaken us, challenged us, and transformed us like the events of September eleventh. Our way of life is now changed forever. The world looks different now. More than seeing through a glass darkly, we look through the lens of terror. We are paused upon the precipice of panic, waiting for the other shoe to drop.

I do not care how heavy your study Bible, how gold-encrusted your cross, or how tight your halo, everybody stood still for a moment as fear tried to eat through the fabric of your faith, like moths locked in a wool factory! We started to sing what the hymnologist wrote generations ago: "I don't know about tomorrow, I just live from day to day."

These events force us to examine our lives more effectively than our usual planned periods of reflection, such as New Year's, Christmas, Thanksgiving, marriages, deaths, and firings or hirings. In fact, there is no better time than right now to take inventory. This is a good time to examine our human relationships, values, belief systems, priorities, and especially our relationship with Jesus Christ.

Isn't it amazing that what was important on September tenth becomes a moot issue when you look at the smoldering New York City skyline?

On September tenth you were comfortable about putting off until tomorrow what you needed to do that day. Not anymore when you consider that nearly six thousand people have no tomorrow.

The complaints you had about where you worked lost wind when you consider you could have been working on the one-hundred-fourth floor of the World Trade Center or at the Pentagon.

Going somewhere was important because you never got to go anywhere because of too much work and too little money—until you remember you could have been on any one of those doomed air carriers.

Our heroes were those who could run faster, jump higher, hit the hardest, score the most runs, baskets, or touchdowns, playing the game better than any other human on the face of the earth—and getting paid millions to do it. Now our heroes are those who stay behind to help victims to safety, losing their lives to save others.

Our home looks a lot better. We want to hug our children, wives, husband, and friends a lot more. We won't forget again to say, "I love you" to those you really love. We are finally going to break down and get that cell phone.

We are thinking about our wills, estates, and insurance policies, getting our houses in order just in case we go from earth to glory so quickly and so tragically!

The tapestry of the twenty-first century has been stained with innocent blood. Our faith tradition teaches us that vengeance belongs to the Lord, but we would rather do it. We know to pray, but we're still mad. We're taught to "turn the other cheek," but we don't want to. We know we are to return good for evil, but we feel like teaching evil a lesson or two.

The world looks different now. The world feels different. We are forced to examine our role in it while examining our human relationships, values, priorities, belief systems, and especially our relationships with Jesus Christ.

Thank God for the Word of God. The experience of a group of people in the midst of transition may help us this morning as we search for answers in our own season of transition.

The Old Testament account of the Hebrew exodus from slavery in Africa to freedom in the Promised Land is familiar to most of us. A famine arose that created hardships for the people of God in the Fertile Crescent. God worked behind the scenes to get Israel's patriarch, Joseph, into position as Pharaoh's second-in-command—all in spite of his family's attempts to kill him and the whims of masters, jailers, and friends to delay his dream becoming a reality.

In the end the dream God gave Joseph as a boy became a reality, "in the fullness of time" in his maturity. The experiences in-between at Potiphar's house and in prison served to prepare him for his leadership role in the future. He had opportunities to learn how to handle the responsibilities of running a household, of administration, of office politics and personnel, and of managing resources. The testimony is that no matter where Joseph was, God granted him success.

The brothers who had rejected him now were forced by famine to seek his favor. After a tearful reconciliation, the Hebrews left the Fertile Crescent for Egypt. They lived. They prospered. They grew to be a nation within a nation in Goshen.

Then a Pharaoh arose who did not know Joseph. He was not familiar with the genius and grace of Joseph. He was not privy to the greatness of the God of Joseph.

The Egyptians became concerned about the growing minority in Goshen. The strength of the Hebrews could threaten the balance of power in the African nation one day, they worried. In order to control the Hebrews, an involuntary abortion program was established. The midwives were commanded to kill the boys born to the Hebrew women at birth, but to let the girls live.

The midwives Shiphrah and Puah conspired with the mother of Moses to keep him alive. Moses was set adrift on the river in a woven basket of watertight reeds that attracted the attention of Pharaoh's sister. Miriam, the young baby's sister, offered the services of her mother to nurse the baby. Thus, Moses was raised by an unwed surrogate in the sight of his birth mother in Pharaoh's household.

As Pharaoh instituted an economic development plan based upon the free labor of the Hebrews, the people cried out in pain to God. God heard the prayers of the people.

Just as God worked behind the scenes to develop Joseph, so God worked behind the scenes of Moses' life to prepare him for leadership. Moses, the one raised within the enemy's camp, was chosen by God to be the instrument of salvation. The hard heart of Pharaoh was softened by ten plagues, the last being the death of every firstborn. Pharaoh's arrogance opened the door for the death angel to visit his own household. The blood of lambs kept safe the Hebrews in the long dark night of death ... and the death angel passed over them.

As we approach our text we find that Pharaoh has released them—not out of the kindness of his heart, but by God's prompting. God has a way of making his enemies change their minds.

The Hebrews left Egypt to worship God. They traveled along well-worn paths through the wilderness, a choice that perhaps caused them to be easily pursued.

By Exodus 14, Pharaoh begins to thinks about the good ole days. Who is going to supply free labor? Who will weave our fabric, raise our children, make our bricks, build our pyramids, construct our cities, or farm our land? He longed for the way things used to be and pursued the Hebrews into the wilderness.

The Lord spoke to Moses to tell the children of Israel to camp between Migdol and the sea. Perhaps God's people heard the thunder of the hooves of the horses and the wheels of the war chariots. They saw the dust of a great army behind them and they became afraid.

They said to Moses, "Because there were no graves in Egypt, hast thou taken us away to die in the wilderness? wherefore hast thou dealt with us, to carry us forth out of Egypt?" (Exodus 14:11, KJV). They, too, engaged in a desire to return to the good ole days.

The children of Israel were in a season of transition. What was ... was no longer. What will be ... was not yet. The old way of doing things was gone. As tomorrow was on the way, yesterday began to look better.

They had been enslaved, mistreated, abused, and persecuted. Yet they cried out to return to what was rather than face the future. The future was no longer certain. The enemy was following quickly to vanquish them. They were forced to evaluate their values, priorities, and their relationships, even their relationship with God. The conclusion: Let's go back to the way things were, no matter how painful. At least we know what was, because we are afraid of what will be.

We want to go back when what we know about yesterday is better than what we know about today or tomorrow. The children of Israel knew what they had, a home in the mud pits of Goshen. They could content themselves with making bricks without straw and building pyramids. Yesterday they had a bountiful menu. Today they are not sure about the wilderness diet. Yesterday they had a master they could see and serve. Today they had an unseen Lord above them, an army behind them, and a sea in front of them.

They were neither the first nor the last to think such thoughts. Many people in the wake of September 11, 2001 have cried out for the way things used to be, because we are uncertain about the future. The twenty-first century way of living is too frightening. Let's go back to the days when we knew our neighbors, when it was safe to go out at night and everyone knew where their children were at 11 P.M.—the good ole days that were predictable in content, ritual in structure, secure in definitive gender roles, traditional from start to finish, conservative by nature.

Yesterday we know. Dances were less provocative. Strong language was left to sailors and saloons. The worse you could hear were the Redd Foxx and Moms Mabley records your parents kept hidden in the basement.

In the twenty-first century style of living, vulgar is hot, down-and-dirty is in, and the less you wear in strategic locations the better.

Yesterday we know. Men didn't wear earrings or carry purses. The only braiding done in the house was your daughter's, not your son's, hair. Women pierced their ears. Today, women *and* men pierce their tongues, eyebrows, lips, and belly buttons. Tattoos were for sailors and motorcyclists. Now your mother, sister, girlfriend, aunts, uncles, brothers, and ballplayers have tattoos. Yesterday, the worst you could do to your hair was to go blond. Today, Miss Clairol comes in pink, blue, green, yellow, and fire-engine red! Yesterday you just made do with what you had. Today, whatever you do not have you can buy, extend, crimp, curl, cornrow, weave, or wig it.

We want to retreat to our yesterdays when what we knew yesterday is better than what we do and don't know about today. Then, turn in your cell phone, computer, pager, and fax machine, and palm pilot. Give up your microwave, self-cleaning oven, hot water heater, washer and dryer, vacuum cleaner, no-iron sheets, plastic, and Poly-and-Esther (polyester). Yesterday, no power steering, power brakes, power locks, intermittent windshield wipers, automotive navigational systems, airbags, clean-air filters, fog lights, high-performance gas, air conditioning, satellite dishes, Monday Night Football, cable, pay-per-view, laptops, Internet, e-commerce, Home

Shopping Network, or shopping online. Forget about mammograms, miracle drugs, heart and lung machines, laser treatments, and MRIs.

We want to go back to the golden days of yesterday when tomorrow doesn't make sense. When events and experiences do not correspond to anything familiar, we long for the yesterday we know. And the closer we get to tomorrow, the more we want yesterday. If we are not careful we will live with a nostalgic hope that tomorrow will be yesterday.

The Israelites were trapped between the wilderness, the sea, and Pharaoh's approaching army. They had never been in a situation like that before. The exodus had exposed their vulnerability. It appeared foolish to travel so far to die at the water's edge when they could have saved energy and died in Goshen. They no longer had the familiarity of enslavement—depending upon others to make decisions for them, living at the mercy of another's idea of life. They could not depend upon the predictability of their former circumstances. Now, all they could do was depend on God.

When the highjacked airplanes hit their mark, we all felt vulnerable. The chink in our national armor was uncovered. We were at the mercy of a madman's plot to kill and destroy indiscriminately. We felt the impact of the tragedy because we could have easily been on the planes or at Ground Zero. We saw ourselves trying to escape a collapsing building. We were there, running from the dust and rubble. We had friends in those buildings. We know someone who died or was rescued. We remember being there, working there, visiting there yesterday, last week, last month, or years ago.

The tragedy of that Tuesday does not correspond to anything we have ever experienced. It just doesn't make sense.

If all you know is writing a check to pay bills, banking online doesn't make sense. If all you do is purchase stock from a broker, trading online doesn't make sense. If you can barely handle the mail delivered by the U.S. postal system, e-mail doesn't make sense.

If wars are fought in someone else's backyard, America under attack doesn't make sense. If the rules of engagement change from soldiers on the battlefield, sailors on the high seas, and missiles in the air to terrorism, things don't make sense. If you are used to conventional warfare and find yourself in an unconventional conflict, things do not make sense. If you are used to engaging the enemy within their own borders, an enemy without borders doesn't make sense.

Like the children of Israel, we want to go back when the certainty of the past outweighs the uncertainty of the future, when what we knew yesterday seems better than what we know about today. We want to go back to good ole days when tomorrow doesn't make sense, when today has no relationship to past experiences. And we want to abandon the future when change is beyond our control.

Everything was changing for the Israelites all at the same time—environment change, lifestyle change, dietary change, dependency change, economic change, political change, social change.

Tomorrow can be extraordinarily difficult when everyone and everything changes all at the same time. Change was coming for the past four hundred years, but to the Hebrews, it seemed like an overnight sensation. They were working a dead-end job in Egypt and the next thing they knew, they were out in the wilderness on the way to the Promised Land. The change had been wanted and prayed for ... but the change was beyond their control.

We tend to act strangely and strongly to changes beyond our control. Our desire for change may be profound. We may be working toward change or doing the things necessary for change to take place. We want change by our own design, change orchestrated by the human hand and the human mind. God should check with us first before any change takes place.

What happened in Exodus was change orchestrated by God. God never lost control of the event no matter how painful it became.

When we suddenly have to move out of our predictability into unpredictability, all we want to do is return to what used to be, to what was and what we know for sure—even if what we knew was not good, not right, not efficient, not excellent, not trustworthy or valuable. It may not be working, but it is what we know. Or, it just may have always been this way.

On Tuesday, September 11, 2001, when evil was at its worst, God was at his best. God did not lose control of the event.

Our values, priorities, and relationships began to change all at the same time. A nation and a world turned to God. A collective cry rang out and we all dropped to our knees in prayer. Separation of church and state did not matter when the President of the United States called for a day of prayer and mourning. Prayer went forth in schools, businesses, and governments. People prayed openly in the streets.

Who was ashamed of the gospel of Jesus Christ? None! Who was embarrassed to call upon his name? None! Who needed an anchor in this turbulent tragedy? Everyone! What could have taken a generation or two to do was done in one morning.

Churches, synagogues, mosques, and temples filled to capacity. In just one morning, God working within human events to change the world, our nation returned to "One nation under God" and "God bless America!"

Moses inquired of the Lord. The response was swift. "Fear not. Stand still and see the salvation of the Lord."

Cultures change. Circumstances change. People change. Societies change. Policies and politics change. Economic indicators change. Kingdoms (and the stock market) rise and fall. Leaders ascend and descend pulpits and thrones. The scenery and cast of characters change. Morals and mores change.

Fear not, there is one constant. God is immutable and changeless. Jesus is the same yesterday, today, and forever more! The Lord is infinite above our finite human changes. His character and attributes are set. They are not swayed or influenced by human changes. His standards are absolute. The standards are our North Star to help us find our Christian lifestyle. They are the sun, the center of our solar system. God is the one fixed point in our fast-moving drama of life.

Our God works in and through change to accomplish his purpose ... getting us to the promised places in Christ. Our confidence is not in ourselves. Our confidence is not in missiles, tanks, guns, smart bombs, aircraft carriers, or stealth bombers. Our confidence is in the God who created the world and us. As David declares, "Some trust in horses, some trust in chariots, but I trust in God" (Psalm 20:7).

Fear not ... it is wise and safe to trust God. The Lord is trustworthy in every area of your life. Trust God and obey his commands; live according to his wisdom; yield to his guidance; move without hesitation in response to his direction.

"... but I trust in God." Trust God to be your financial advisor, career counselor, and vocation determinator. Trust God to be your personal love advisor, partner locator, matchmaker and dating service. Trust God to be your marriage counselor, parental advisor, peacekeeper, and provider of all your needs. The Promise Maker is the Promise Keeper who can usher you through this valley of terror, uncertainty, and fear.

Now is the time to trust God, as Daniel did, while we are in the den of lions. Trust God like the three Hebrew boys while in the fiery furnace; trust God like Paul and Silas when fear tries to imprison us; trust God like Mary with a surprise pregnancy; trust God like Abraham with our only son; trust God like ole Noah through public ridicule; trust God like David on the battlefield with our giants; trust God like Christ when we hang on our crosses, crucified, waiting for Sunday morning.

Pharaoh and bin Laden may be on your trail. You may be trapped by a wilderness of uncertainty. There is a God who can help you through sense-less times and lead you to power, joy, and a sound mind. God did not give us a spirit of fear.

Moses declared, "Fear not, stand still, and see the salvation of the LORD.... The LORD will fight for you, and ye shall hold your peace." Then the Lord said to Moses, "Why do you stand here crying to me? Tell the people to move forward."

As Bishop Robert Pruitt used to say, as God said to Moses, as Moses said to the people, so I say to you: It is time to move forward. Forward march!

Yesterday is dead and gone. Tomorrow may never come. It is time to look to the horizon of hope. God has not changed his mind. "I know the plans I have for you, plans not to harm but to prosper you." "He who has begun a good work will complete it."

It is time to move forward. Do your business plan. Go house hunting. Plan your wedding. Study for your promotion. Learn how the department works. Reshape your resumé. Go on a diet. Turn off the news. Get your credit together. Go back to school. Learn your supervisor's job. Start a journal. Go online. Make investments; repair your relationships; write for-gotten letters; say thank you; tell the people you love that you love them. Get a haircut, a makeover. Learn to drive; make new friends; get out of the house. Go to the doctor; get the prescription filled; set new long- and short-term goals. Get your act together, but for God's sake, *move forward!*

Now is not the time to sound a retreat. Now is the time to move forward.

We have a war to fight. This war is not fought with carnal weapons of war but with spiritual weapons. This is not the deployment of armaments and ammunition but the unleashing of heaven's arsenal. This war is not fought on foreign soil but in our own hearts, minds, and souls.

This is a war declared on hatred. What we saw September eleventh is the same hatred that built ovens in Auschwitz; the same hatred that hung black fruit from Southern trees; the same hatred that justifies ethnic cleansing; the same hatred that permits children to be enslaved; the same hatred that encourages children to kill children in cold blood; the same hatred that removes the blindfold from the eyes of justice; and the same hatred that bombs children on their way to school in Ireland.

The hatred we are seeing has been reformulated for the twenty-first century, but it is not new. We have a real opportunity to move forward in our own country and to lead the world to declare war on this hatred. It is a war fought and won on our knees, one heart at a time. It is a personal war that has public implications. People of God, it is time to move forward.

Seeking God's Face

William D. Watley

SEPTEMBER 16, 2001

"Come," my heart says, "seek his face!" Your face, LORD, do I seek.

—Psalm 27:8, NRSV

Some of us are blessed to be here this morning, truly blessed to be here. If you were either in that building, in any of those buildings, or in the vicinity and could have been in those buildings, stand. If you should have been over there and something stopped you from going, interfered with your going on Tuesday, would you stand? [Several persons stand.] Amen. It's a blessing to be here.

Seeking God's face. Note that the psalmist does not say, "Come, my heart says, SEE his face, your face, Lord, do I SEE." But "Come," my heart says, "SEEK his face." The psalmist says, "'Come,' my heart says, 'seek his face.' Your face, LORD, do I seek." The question occurs to me: Why does the psalmist have to SEEK God's face? I mean, if as our ancestors used to say, God really is so high that you can't get over him and so wide that you can't get around him and so low that you can't get under him, why do you have to SEEK God's face? If to seek God's face means to have the actual experience of God's manifest presence not only in the world but in our own individual lives—like we like to testify that he woke us up this morning, started us on our way—then why do we have to SEEK God? He ought to be so big and obvious that we shouldn't have to seek him. I mean before the Twin Towers of the World Trade Center fell, you didn't have to seek them. All you had to do was look at the Manhattan skyline and they were there so obviously you could see them without straining. So why is it that we have to seek a big God?

I would submit to you this morning that as big as God is and as powerful as God is, there are times and experiences in our lives when we don't really see God or feel God's hand of presence or understand what God is doing and can't see where God is working stuff out. Even some of the strongest believers in the Scripture had times in their life when they really felt God's absence more than God's presence. That's what Job was talking about when he said, "Oh, that I knew where I might find him that I might come to his seat. If I go forward he is not there, if I go backwards I cannot perceive him, to the left he hides and to the right I cannot see him." That's what even David was talking about in Psalm 42:1-3, when he says, "As a deer pants for the stream, so my soul thirsts for God, the living God. When shall I come and behold your face? My tears have been my food day and night while my enemies continually ask me in the midst of my trouble where is your God?" The prophet Habakkuk had trouble at times connecting with God. That's why he begins that great prophecy by saying, "How long do I have to cry for you to help and you do not save and how long do I cry violent and you do nothing? Your eyes are too pure to look upon evil and treachery and wrongdoing and yet you allow those who are innocent to suffer at the hands of evil." Even the Lord Jesus Christ at times felt God's absence. Remember the great prayer he prayed on Calvary, "My God, my God, why have you forsaken me?"

There are times when all of us, no matter how big and powerful and close our walk with the Lord, feel the absence of God in our situation. Don't ever let anybody tell you that trouble makes you stronger and trouble makes you more righteous. There are sometimes when the devil can put stuff in your life and trouble can come when you don't feel close to God. There are times in your life when the enemy can assault you with so much, hell breaks loose all around you everywhere you look and you have to wonder, God, where am I and where are you?

This experience is causing some people to feel disconnected from God. There are some people who are walking around today asking God, Why? Why did you allow this to happen to us, right now in this place and at this time? There are some people who were blessed to survive, but were so traumatized by the event that they continue to relive it in their spirit and say, "God, I'm thankful, but I still have trouble connecting with you right during this period." There are people who made it, but they're saying, "God, I'm grateful for my life, but I don't know about my future. Now I don't know what's gonna happen with the company that I work for and does that mean that I'm going to have to start over and begin anew at this point in my life?" There are people who were saved and who still feel guilty because they have loved ones and friends and family members who are lost. And they're saying to God, "I'm grateful, but why me and what about them?" And there are people who even now are praying and fasting for people to be saved and delivered and God's gonna say no. And when God says no, they're gonna be saying, "God, you did it for others. What about my child and my husband and wife, and my mother and father, my brother and sister, my best friend? Why couldn't you save them?"

I repeat, there are experiences that can shake all of us to the core. And that's why we have to be careful about how self-righteous and judgmental we become when others are going through their struggle and tell them that they ought to be stronger and that they ought to believe. There are some times when no matter how much you try, you just don't have it. The devil has stuff planned, and you never know when trouble is going to fall on your doorstep. And the same thing that you told somebody else—they had to be strong—will hit you with such a vengeance.

When I was out of work for an eight-month period, my father said that he was not worried about me getting another job. He said he knew that would happen. He said what he was most concerned about was me losing my preaching gift. He said that because there were a couple of times during that period when I stood up to preach and he said I just didn't have it. And he was right. Because that was a season when I had so much anger with God and so many questions of God and so many issues with God that I couldn't really connect with God. And so when I stood up to preach I didn't have any power to deliver. There are times when trouble can so disorient us and so disconnect us that we don't have the power on our own to stand and keep standing, especially when we are innocent and have done nothing to really deserve suffering. I mean, Job was pronounced by God as being a man who was upright and blameless in his ways. When somebody needed to replace King Saul, who had fallen from favor, God said that David was the man after his own heart. When Jesus was baptized, the heavens opened up and the Holy Spirit spoke and said, "This one is mine, in whom I am well pleased, hear ye him." And yet, as righteous and as close and as anointed and as faithful as they were, there were times when they did not feel the presence and the power of God in their lives.

Habbakuk had a different issue. Habbakuk was upset because of what had happened to his people. And even though he recognized that the people of Israel had fallen short of the glory of God and were in exile in Babylon, he also recognized that the Chaldeans who were oppressing them were also heathen and pagan and did not know the God of Israel. And while we condemn the dastardly, vile, and vicious act perpetrated against those people who were innocent at the World Trade Center—and while there ought to be an appropriate response—the fact of the matter—and this is a prophetic word that's gonna be hard for some of us to hear—the fact of the matter is that it's a wake-up call on this nation. We have been too arrogant and abusive of others in the way that we have dealt with power. We have used our power to undermine governments, and then used our weapons to put people in power who support our interests. And now the same people that we trained, and the same weapons that we provided, are being turned back against us. Martin Luther King said it right in 1967, one year to the date before his death, when he stood up in the Riverside Church in his "Time to Break Silence" speech and came out against the war in Vietnam. He said then that we were on the wrong side of a worldwide revolution of colored and oppressed people. And we have not changed our position since. The colored and Third World peoples do not look upon us as their friend but as their enemy. And it's time that we as a nation humble ourselves and repent. We should not have walked out of the UN Conference on racism and xenophobia. When apartheid was ruling in South Africa, Israel did support it, and so did our government. We only backed sanctions late in the game, and we did it over the objection of

Ronald Reagan, who was in office, and the Republicans, who were in power. That's not partisan politics, that's truth. And it means that we need to re-think and re-examine the ways we have done foreign policy and immigration policy in the past. There is something wrong when the people you train fire at us with the weapons we give them. We persecute Haitians. Haitians have nothing. They come over here on rafts or anything they can with empty hands and we lock them up and we open the doors for others with straighter hair. And the ones that we have opened the doors for have used our own training fields. It is time that this nation repent. If my people...that's the only way healing is going to come. It will not come by might nor by power. That's why we gotta seek God's face.

I mean, God is saying to us, be clear. Some trust in horses and some trust in chariots, but our security will not rest in our internal or external systems of defense. You don't have enough firepower to go against the midnight, guerilla-fighting terrorists. The only thing that keeps us is the Lord God Jehovah. And that's why we gotta seek God's face. And I know that ain't easy sometimes, but sometimes we've just got to be honest and open with the Lord. And forget all of those fancy textbook prayers. Forget all of that! Sometimes we just got to get real down and dirty and say, "God, I got some problems. I got some problems with you, I got anger in me, I got questions in me, I got doubt in me, I'm carrying guilt and grief. I don't know what you are doing and sometimes, God, I don't even know if you exist! But God, I got faith the size of a mustard seed. Oh Hallelujah! And your word told me that you could take my mustard seed faith and that you can move mountains. So here I am, God. I'm bringing my mountain of problem, my mountain of perplexity, my mountain of burdens, my mountain of guilt, my mountain of questions, my mountain of pain and anger. And I'm asking you to do what you do best: to take my mustard seed faith and move these mountains. Oh, yeah. I know that you can, and I believe that you will. And when it's all over, I don't want to be in stress. I want to have strength."

"Come, my heart says, seek, seek." There are some things that a self-help book can't give you. There are some things that good therapy and advice can't do for you. There are some things that other folk can't do for you. David says, "Come, my heart says, seek." I don't care how difficult it is, seek it anyhow. Even when you don't feel him, seek him anyhow. We might not feel him, but he feels you. That's what he told to Moses: that I have seen the oppression of my people in Egyptian fields and I myself have come down. They've been praying a long time, and I know they thought that I hadn't heard them, but I'm still God, I'm still in charge, I still rule, not Pharoah! Seek his face and pray through. How are we gonna' make it? Job declared it when he finished questioning God. He said that God knows the path that I take and when he shall have tried me, I shall come forth like pure gold. David understood, when he got through questioning God, he said, "I would have fainted unless I had believed to see the goodness of the Lord in the land of the living. Wait on the Lord and he shall strengthen thine heart, wait on the Lord." "Why are thou disquietest? Hope thou in God and you will again praise him." Habbakuk asked his questions, but he prayed his way through. He went up to his prayer tower and came back with affirmation. Although the fig tree does not blossom, neither shall there be fruit on the vine and the fruit of the olive shall fail. There shall be no herd in the stall, yet I will rejoice in the Lord, I will joy in the God of my salvation. He makes my feet like hind's feet and calls me to stand in high and lofty places. Jesus told us—he said that after he prayed, "My God, my God"—why he turned his face toward heaven, not at those folk who were persecuting him, not at those folk who denied him or betrayed him or mocked him or spit at him or spat upon him. He looked at God and said, "Even on the cross I know I'm still in your hand. Father, into your hands..."How are we going make it? Seek his face.

There was a father and his little girl. They had just buried his wife and her mother. She was a little bitty thing, three or four years old. And that night after all the relatives had gone, this father put his little girl in bed and turned out the light and kissed her and went and got in his own bed. About ten minutes later he heard his daughter's voice calling him from the foot of his bed. She said, "Daddy, I'm scared." He said, "Why are you scared, pudding?" She said. "Because it's dark, daddy." And the daddy said, "I know it's dark." And the little girl said, "Daddy, it's darker than it's ever been." And she said, "Can I get in bed with you?" He said, "Sure baby." And he picked her up and put the little girl in the spot where her mother used to sleep and turned off the light. Two minutes later he heard the little girl say, "Daddy?" "Yeah, baby." "I can't see your face. Are you looking at me? Is your face turned toward me?" And the father said, "Yes, baby, my face is turned toward you." And the little girl went to sleep in peace because she knew that her father's face was turned toward her.

I don't know what the future holds. Sometimes it will get darker than it's ever been. But even in the darkness, know that your father's face... Sometimes you will not get a prayer through and sometimes you'll be broken in spirit and all you can say is God have mercy upon me. But even then know that your father's face is turned toward you. And sometimes you'll get confused and don't know which way to go, and sometimes mean people will do mean things to you and it will break your heart. But just remember, when other folk act unkindly toward you, that your father's face, oh hallelujah, is still turned toward you. And we know that this morning that that's the only reason that we have made it. When contentious tongues cast our names out as evil, our father's face still looked at us and blessed us and gave us the victory.

Proclaim Peace
in Times
Like These

Meeting God Again, the First Time

Charles G. Adams

September 16, 2001

Be still, and know that I am God.   —Psalm 46:10, KJV

L ast Tuesday is a day that shook the world as we know it, and I believe it now forces the world either to find the God who created the world or cling to the anti-god, to violence, which aims to destroy the world, a world that is in a suspended stage where God and the creatures of God outwardly project and act out what is in their hearts and in their souls. Consider yourself today an actor upon the stage of the world. The world you're in is a world that you have the power to move, to act upon, to make a difference in, either for good or evil, for God or for the enemy, for truth or error, for falsehood, deception, and destruction or for salvation.

Last Tuesday changed our sense of security in the world forever. Never again will we underestimate the power of what we don't know to crash every system of human security that we have taken for granted. Never again will we climb into an airplane or ride in a car or sit in an office or step out on the street or even stay in bed without questioning the adequacy of our security. We will always be wondering whether or not we are really safe anywhere in the world, a world where we share one stage with billions of people—interconnected, interactive, interdependent, interrelated people, people we do not know—and with trillions of thoughts that we do not understand in terms of their ability to smite or to heal.

Tuesday, 9.11.01, we found that the thoughts of misguided people turned nonviolent domestic aircraft into guided missiles of destruction. There came to the world, not a gentle knock at the door, but a crude, rude, and violent awakening, an awakening to the fact of our vulnerability and insecurity in a strange world. Tuesday, we were shaken out of our routines and forced to confront the fact that what you don't believe *can* hurt you. And what you don't know *can* kill you.

Last Tuesday morning there came a sobering of the nation and a quieting of the world. The streets are not as noisy; the music is not as loud; business is not so brisk. There is a slowing down. There is a quieting down. There is a standing still; there is an inner call to question quietly who we are, where we are, why we are, and what we are to do. Somebody has shaken us up. Somebody has shaken up America. Somebody has awakened the world. Somebody has gotten our attention. Somebody has shattered our delusions of invincibility, invulnerability, and indestructibility. Somebody is knocking at the door. Somebody is shouting in our ear. Somebody is calling in our hearts. Somebody is speaking in our souls, like in the words of Psalm 46:10: "Be still, and know that I am God" (KJV).

The explosions and destruction of last Tuesday have torn down the curtain of private confidence and driven us openly onto the stage where people are moving and acting, demonstrating who they really are, what they really think, and whom they really trust. These are the times that do not just *try* our souls. These are the times that *define* our souls, that determine our character, that demonstrate who we really are. Shakespeare said, "What a mighty work is man." The psalmist said: "What is man?" Who are mortals, vulnerable human beings, that God is actually mindful of us, really cares about us, is speaking to us, calling to us, summoning us to look up and come up to a higher level of life, a better way of love, a finer way of being?

Even children have been awakened, even little children living in the world of play and pleasure and privilege are sharing their toys, donating their stuffed animals to comfort the suffering little brothers and sisters whose parents have disappeared. My son, Christian, said that he was moved to tears when his little boy was watching television, and instead of looking at the cartoons that day, instead of watching Mr. Rogers, he saw people wounded and crying and covered with dust and running for their lives, trying to get away from the fires and explosions and destruction all around them. And he said, "Daddy, I hope those people are gonna be all right." I hope and I pray that all of us will be all right, that all of us will choose the way of love and not hate, sympathy and not indifference, peace and not violence, compassion and not anger, hope and not despair, forgiveness and not revenge.

These are the times that define our selfhood, that drive us to name our God out of the dust and debris of our broken hopes and shattered illusions. We've been flying about without even thinking about God. We've been running and rushing around without contemplation, meditation, or appreciation. We don't have time. Many of us don't have time to pray, don't have time to come to church, don't have time to open a Bible, don't have time to be still, don't have time even to love our neighbors.

Acquaint now thyself with God. Be still and know that God is. But we have so many escape systems to get away from God. Lust for power is an escape system. Work can be an escape system. Noise certainly is an escape system to keep us from hearing the voice of God. Stop trying to avoid God. Stop putting God on hold, severing the connection between the creature and the Creator, the mind and the Maker, the soul and the Savior.

We have turned up the boom boxes so high that we can't hear the challenge of truth, the stirrings of consciencce, or the still, small voice of God. We couldn't hear before Tuesday, but we're hearing now. We were too busy before Tuesday, but we're not quite so busy now. Oh, some of us were too selfish to share before Tuesday. Some of us were too bothered to care before Tuesday. And then, boom, boom, boom, boom. Four explosions silenced our noise, stopped us in our tracks, brought civilization to a screeching halt, canceled our selfish celebrations, postponed all of our fun and games, shattered our walls of separation, shut down the stock market, put brakes on our foolish talk shows, suspended our tasteless humor, silenced all of our midnight mockeries of truth, put on hold all of those maddening episodes that we have followed, looking for more fun, more frivolity, and finding only more futility. But all we could see Tuesday were the crumbling buildings, falling idols, and hurting people—a civilization under the siege of chaos, terrorism, and inhumanity.

Tuesday will go down as the day that changed the world. Tuesday, all of our escape systems were blocked, and all of our evasions were shut off by the reality of adversity. I do not believe that God caused those explosions of Tuesday. I do not believe that God does evil. But I do believe that God can use anything and will use everything to get our attention, to speak to our souls, and to deliver us from the evil that has come upon us and that settles within us.

There are three realities that speak to us from the dust and smoke and wreckage of these times. Number one, the reality of God. How is it that we come to find the reality of God in the rubble and wreckage of our failed hopes and shattered dreams? You know, sometimes—not all the time but sometimes—God has a way of causing everything in your life and my life to be moved that can be moved so that what cannot be moved will be seen as that which needs to stand and remain and continue, even though everything else has fallen away.

Now you don't believe that, but in Hebrews, the twelfth chapter and the twenty-fifth verse, we read this:

See that you do not refused the one who is speaking; for if they did not escape when they refused the one who warned them on earth, how much less will we escape if we reject the one who warns from heaven! At that time his voice shook the earth; but now he has promised, "Yet once more I will shake not only the earth but also the heaven." This phrase, "Yet once more," indicates the removal of what is shaken—that is, created things—so that what cannot be shaken may remain. (NRSV)

You know that will happen in your life. Everything that can be shaken will be shaken. Everything that can fail will fail in order that that which cannot be shaken and that which shall never fail will remain. That's what happened to Job. Everything in his life crumbled. All of his prosperity was destroyed. All of his children were killed. All of his security was shattered. All of his friends failed. His government broke down, his culture was shattered, his education failed, his health was destroyed, his world collapsed, his theology proved to be insufficient, inadequate, and incomplete. And he sat stripped and naked before God. No more deceptions, no more delusions of grandeur, no more illusions of security or invincibility. All he had was God, but that was enough!

Tuesday happened to short-circuit the false security of our world and to show us that, in the final analysis, when you strip away all the confusions and illusions of our boasting, all we really have and all we can truly depend on and all we can really be sure of is God. That's all we have, just God. That's all and that's enough. Because that's everything that's real, everything that's true, and everything that's reliable. God! In the person of Jesus. God! In the power of the Holy Spirit. God! In the courage to be. God! In the strength to love. God! In the soul, in the world, working in everything that happens to make it come out like it should so we can say, "All things work together for good for those who love God, who are called according to his purpose" (Romans 8:28, NRSV).

God is our refuge and strength, a very present help in trouble.
Therefore we will not fear, though the earth should change,
    though the mountains shake in the heart of the sea,
though its waters roar and foam,
    though the mountains tremble with its tumult.
               —Psalm 46:1-4, NRSV

The Lord of hosts is with us. The God of Jacob is our refuge. Come and behold the works of the Lord. Come and behold the works of the creatures of God. What desolations have been made around the world. Come to Pennsylvania. Come to New York. Come to Washington; visit the Pentagon. Come to the cities of America. Come to the crumbling cities of the world, to impoverished nations where AIDS and war, sickness and poverty, capitalistic globalization, pain and revenge, all ravage the whole continent of Africa, shatter the whole culture of Afghanistan, exploit the cheap labor of Indonesia, exclude the poor people of Pakistan, crowd out the Aborigines of Australia. Come and see God at work in places where we have been told that God is absent, that God is not at work.

Come, behold the works of the Lord. He makes wars to cease to the end of the earth. He breaks the bow. He shatters the spear. He burns the chariot in fire. He speaks to every person, every race, every religion, every nation: "Be still, sit down, and know that I am God."

God says clearly, "Not you, but *I* will be exalted among the nations. I will be exalted in the earth." When your buildings fall and your culture is shattered and your illusions are broken, your securities fail, you will still find God. You will still see Jesus. You will still receive the gift of the Spirit and the courage to go on anyhow. You will know who is in charge, and you will learn how to sing "God is our refuge and strength, a very present help in trouble." The security has failed. The Pentagon is damaged. The Twin Towers have crumbled. But still, God is God. And God is love and God is hope and God is life. The Lord of hosts is with us. The God of Jacob is our refuge. We've got to find God in all this turmoil. We better see God in all the wreckage and in the ruin of false security and worthless wealth.

And right next to the reality of God, there is the inevitability of pain. And that we think to be a contradiction of terms. If God is love, why is there still hate? Why is there still violence? Why is there still evil in a world that God made and God sustains and God orders and governs? If God is perfect—and God is—and Job is blameless, why is there suffering in the life of Job and in this world? Read Genesis 1-3, and you will see there that God created the world, not out of nothing, but out of chaos. God created everything good, brought us to it, put us in it, and we messed it up. We exploited what we should have appreciated. We consumed what we should have preserved. We messed up what we should have maintained.

Satan didn't make us. Satan can't rule us. We have got to come to the point that we stop talking to Satan and start talking to God. Don't be so satanically preoccupied that you lose your heavenly confidence, your eternal security, and your spiritual anointing. Nobody can empower Satan but you. Nobody can mess up your mind but you. And nobody can ride your back unless you bend it! But we invited Satan into our Garden of Eden, and then we empower Satan every day with our belief in Satan. In a world that we have infected by our foolishness, there is liable to be trouble. There will be an inevitability of suffering in a world that we allow Satan to rule. There will be predators in the Garden, tragedy in human experience, hostility between nations, violence between races, and division between people who need each other and ought to love each other.

But God's still there. God is still good, God is still in charge. And God does not show God's power by stamping out evil. You know, that's the way we'd do it. "I'm gonna stamp it out like it's a cockroach. Stamp it out."

You can stamp all you want. When you get through stamping, you will find that the very evil you thought you stamped out has already risen up in you. God does not stamp out evil, but God takes evil, transforms it, and turns it around on itself, stands it up on its head, and uses it for good. So Satan may mean it for evil, but God will use it for good. And that's exactly what God is doing. God is building up prayer meetings all around. God is showing us the power of love, the power of good will. We are hearing some singing voices, we are listening to some wonderful sermons on television. We see praying spirits all over the world. I'm sure Satan didn't know it. Satan thought that he could break our spirit. Instead Satan caused houses of prayer all over the world to be filled in the name of God.

The planes crashed and the buildings fell, but God is not through with us yet. God is going to bring out of all of this our unity as a people, our faith as believers, our love as neighbors, our life as a body of Christ, and our strength as a nation. Somebody did it for evil, but God is using it right now for good.

Oh, it's a wonderful thing when God takes over. And I hope my dear president will not blow it. And I hope that I don't blow it. And I hope you don't blow it by trying to stamp out the evil that is out there without correcting the evil that is in here. There's some evil in us that we've got to pray for, we've got to ask God to remove. And while you're talking about stamping out Osama bin Laden, don't you think for one minute because you kill him you're gonna kill terrorism. Evil is bigger than him. And evil is also in here, in us. Our own delusions of grandeur, our own prancing, our own puny pretensions and perversions, our own deficiencies of ethics, our own feelings of invincibility. We really don't have to bomb Afghanistan, because if we bomb all those people we'll be no better than the ones who bombed us. God said, "Don't mimic evil; don't repeat wrong." Evil is universal, but God is also everywhere. We cannot go from God's Spirit; we cannot flee from God's presence. If we ascend into heaven, God is there. If we make our beds in hell, God is there. If we live, God is there. If we die, God is there. If we're safe, God is there. If we're in trouble, God is there. And even if we take the wings of the morning and flee to uttermost parts of the sea, even there God will lead us and God's hand will hold us.

Find God in tragedy and you'll be better than you were before the tragedy ever occurred. You know you hear a lot of foolish talk. Somebody said this thing that happened spells the total and complete failure of the United States security system. I said, Say what? You know anybody can complain over one failure, but it takes a genuine child of God to thank God daily for all the things that did not happen that *could* have happened if God had not been watching over us every day. I don't like what the president and founder of the Potomac Institute for Policy Studies, a nonpartisan think tank said. He said, "The time for good diplomacy and sanctions is over. We are at war. This is an intelligence community failure. Their job is to prevent Pearl Harbors. Obviously they failed this time." Joseph Nigh, dean of the Kennedy School of Government at Harvard and a former top Pentagon official, said that the terrorist strikes reflected a massive intelligence failure. But at a forum convened in Cambridge to study the attacks, Nigh added: "We don't always know about the intelligence successes; we only hear about the failures." Their job is to prevent Pearl Harbors. They failed us *this* time. But when was Pearl Harbor? Anybody remember? December 7, 1941. How long ago was that? About sixty years. So, there comes one failure on 9.11.01, and we say that the whole system has failed, forgetting those sixty years that the bombs didn't fall and sixty years that we have had security in this country, and the television programs were not interrupted and the games were not called off. Sure they blew up the Trade Center years ago but that didn't stop the football games. Pearl Harbors were stopped for sixty years, and there was no interruption in our travel plans or our party plans.

And why is it we are so busy talking about one huge failure that we forget to thank God for all the security that we have had? Listen, four flights were hijacked, four planes. Do you know how many flights there are a day? Thirty-five thousand! You know how many days in the year? Three hundred sixty-five. So we're gonna go crazy over one failure when God has kept us through 35,000 flights a day, 365 days a year, for sixty years?

Do you see how foolish we are? When one thing goes wrong, we give up hope. When one thing goes wrong, we go crazy! Anybody can complain about one thing that has gone wrong and the fact that we don't have any security anymore. But the security that we really have cannot be torn. The security that we really have cannot be broken. Oh, I know that it's remotely possible that a plane will come crashing into here in the next five minutes and we will not get home today. That is possible, but not probable. Where do your probabilities come from? I don't know about yours, but mine come from God. So we should never lose hope. The Twin Towers disappeared, but there are some other things still standing tall. St. Patrick's Cathedral is still there; St. John the Divine Cathedral, Riverside Church, Abbysinian, Canaan Baptist, Shiloh, Concord Baptist, Bethany, St. Paul Community Baptist, Cornerstone, Convent Avenue, and Hartford Memorial—all still in New York. The Statue of Liberty is still standing.

But I want you to go a little further than that. Suppose even they fall. Suppose they burn down all the churches and all the mosques and synagogues and praying houses in the world and break down the Statue of Liberty. They can take down the houses of prayer, but they can't silence prayer, defeat hope, destroy love, or stop God. They can take down the Statue of Liberty, but they can't take down liberty. Liberty will be defended, evil will be deterred, peace will be advanced, love will be demonstrated, Christ will be proclaimed, praises will go up, blessings will come down, and we shall overcome together.

So I bid you trust in God. Let us hold hands across racial and ethnic and religious differences and remember that we already have a guarantee that evil is defeated and God is enthroned. Jesus is God's devoted determination always to be with you no matter what. Jesus is God's love that never fails and God's life that never ends. Not that chaos didn't try to destroy God. Chaos stepped in the midst of creation one Friday afternoon on a hill shaped like a bony skull. Chaos tried to be in control. Chaos tried to defeat God. Chaos made the sun fail as it burned out like a cinder. Chaos made the moon hemorrhage and turn red like blood. Chaos made the stars disappear and fall down in a purple haze. Chaos made the earth go crazy and reel like a drunken universe. Chaos threw the world into convulsions as the land vomited up its righteous dead. Right was nailed to the scaffold. Wrong was propped up on the throne. Caesar was set up in the palace. Jesus was nailed to the cross. Innocence was crucified. Guilt was glorified. Love was slain. Hate was heightened. Darkness was ruling. Life was ruined. Evil was reigning. Justice was denied.

But, look what God did with all of that evil. God took all of that evil and used meanness in order to bring about justice. He created your salvation. He created my salvation. God took raw chaos and verified Descartes's intuition. Magnified Hegel's law. Clarified Plato's idea. Satisfied Socrates's question. Purified Kant's categories. Justified Abraham's faith. Gratified Amos's justice. Fortified Hosea's love. Sanctified Micah's mercy. Beautified Ezekiel's vision. Edified Job's confidence. Glorified the whole of creation. Rectified the whole world. Qualified the human race.

He died to make us holy, let us live to make folks free. And God's truth will march on, and we shall all overcome. Trust in God. Believe in God. Hold on to God's unchanging hand, and I declare we'll come out better than we were before Tuesday. Better than we were before the Towers fell, in order for faith, hope, and love to remain.

Outer Turmoil, Inner Strength

Peter J. Gomes

September 23, 2001

Set a straight course and keep to it, and do not be dismayed in the face of
adversity.   —Ecclesiasticus 2:2, REB

M y text is the second verse of the second chapter of the book of
Ecclesiasticus, and the lesson from which it was taken was read in the Revised English Version; I am now taking the King James translation of that
same opening verse, which says: "Set thy heart aright, and constantly endure, and make not haste in time of calamity."

Let me begin with an observation, one might say, of comparative religion. I understand that in the traditions and liturgies of the Greek Orthodox Church, our brethren in the east, when a child is baptized—and by
"child" I mean an infant, not a squalling seven-year-old but a real infant,
literally still damp—in that church, after the baptism has been performed,
the minister or priest or bishop takes his very large pectoral cross (twice the
size of mine) and forcefully strikes the little child on its breast. Strikes it so
hard that it leaves a mark, and so hard that it hurts the child and the child
screams. In the West, we give the child roses. What is the difference here?

The symbolism of the Eastern baptism is clear, indicating that the child
who has been baptized into Christ must bear the cross, and that the cross
is a sign not of ease or of victory or of prosperity or of success, but of

sorrow, suffering, pain, and death. And by it, those things are overcome. It is important to remember that. The symbol of our Christian faith is this very cross that you see on that holy table, carved in that choir screen, worn around the necks of many of us, and held in honor and esteemed by all of us. And it stands to remind us of the troubles of the world that placed our Savior upon it for sins that he did not commit. We Christians, therefore, like those Greek Orthodox babies, ought to expect trouble, turmoil, and tribulation as the normal course of life. We don't, however, because we have been seduced by a false and phony version of the Christian faith which suggests that by our faith we are immune to trouble.

Because we have been nice to God, our thinking goes, then God should be nice to us. Because you have interrupted your normal routine and come here today, God should somehow take note of it, mark it down in the book, and spare you any trouble, tribulation, turmoil, or difficulty. Tribulation, we know, happens only to bad people. Should it, therefore, be happening in spades to all those people who are not here this morning but just getting up out of bed, recovering from a night of pleasure and satiety? Tribulation happens only to the nonobservant and the bad people, and when, as Rabbi Kushner so famously and quite profitably noted, bad things happen to good people, we feel that something has gone terribly wrong. God is not supposed to behave that way, we think, for that is not part of the deal. And we ask, "Where is God?"

Now, let me hasten to say that the answer to that conundrum is not a false conception of God. The issue has nothing whatsoever to do with the so-called death of God, and everything to do with the life and the faith of the believer. It is not the death of God that should concern us; it is the questionable state of the life of the believer. God does not spare us from turmoil. Even the most casual observance of the Scriptures tells us that God strengthens us for turmoil. It is a shabby faith that suggests that God is to do all the heavy lifting and that you and I are to do none. The whole record of Scripture from Genesis to Revelation and the whole experience of the people of God from Good Friday down to and beyond Tuesday, September 11, suggest that faith is forged on the anvil of human adversity. No adversity, no faith.

Consider the lessons we heard this morning. The first lesson, read for us from one of the ancient books of the Jews, the Book of Ecclesiasticus in the Apocrypha, could it be put any plainer? "My son, if thou comest to serve the Lord, prepare thy soul for temptation. Set thy heart aright, and constantly endure, and do not make haste in time of calamity." You don't need a degree in Hebrew Bible or exegesis to figure out what that is saying. What is the context for these words? Trouble, turmoil, tribulation, and temptation: that's the given, that's the context. What is the response for calamity? Endurance. Don't rush, don't panic. What are we to do in calamitous times? We are to slow down. We are to inquire. We are to endure. Tribulation does not invite haste; it invites contemplation, reflection, perseverance, endurance.

Where may we turn for examples of what I am trying to say that the Scriptures say to us? We are in the middle of the great "Days of Awe," with the beginning of the Jewish New Year and the Day of Atonement. And when the Jewish people celebrate these Days of Awe and begin their new year and atone for their sins, they always remember two things. First, they remember the troubles and the tribulations through which they have been, and they recite the history, not of their victories, but of their sorrows and their troubles. They remind themselves and everybody else how they have been formed and forged through the experience of trial and tribulation. They remember those things.

The second thing they remember is how the Lord delivered them out of those troubles and helped them to endure and eventually overcome them. They are reminded of that, and they remind themselves of it over and over and over again. And, when it is said that "It is not the Jew who keeps the law, but the law which keeps the Jew," it is to this process of remembrance, endurance, and deliverance that the aphorism speaks. Again, it says in the Book of Ecclesiasticus, "Look at the generations of old, and see. Whoever did put his trust in the Lord, and was ashamed? Or who did abide in his fear, and was forsaken? Or who did call upon him, and he despised him?" The history of the Jews in the world is not a history of escape from trouble. Would that it were, but it is not! It is the record of endurance through tribulation, an endurance which would have been impossible without God. If any people had the right to claim that 'God was dead,' or at least on sabbatical, it was the Jews, but they never have said it, and they never will, for they know better. They do not worship a metaphor or a simile or a theological construct. They worship the one who stands beside them and who has been with them from Egypt to Auschwitz and beyond, and who enables them to stand up to all that a world of tribulation can throw at them. If we want to know about outer turmoil and inner strength we need look no farther than to our neighbors the Jews. Remember, they wrote the book on the subject.

We may also look a little closer to home. We may look to the authentic witness of the Christian faith to which we bear, in this church, unambiguous allegiance. We do not just believe in God in general, or in a spiritual hope: we believe in Jesus Christ, who is all that we can fully know about God. So, we look at this tradition for inner strength in the midst of outer turmoil.

Consider St. Paul, a Jew and a Christian, and consider his view of things in a less than agreeable world. I hope you heard that second lesson read this morning in J. B. Phillips's pungent prose. Listen to what St. Paul says: "We are handicapped on all sides"—a very fashionable translation of the word, but apt—"but we are never frustrated. We are puzzled," he says, "but never in despair. We are persecuted, but we never have to stand it alone, and"—this fourth part is the part I like the most—"we may be knocked down, but we are never knocked out."

Now Paul is not an abstract theologian, like so many of my colleagues. Paul speaks from the experience of a frustrated but not defeated believer. This is not the sort of "How to be Leaders and Win" sort of stuff that he writes; this is not the kind of CEO book that they trot out in the business school and in motivational seminars. No. Paul writes out of failure, frustration, and conflict, but never out of despair. If you are looking for something to read in these troublesome times, do not turn to books of cheap inspiration and handy-dandy aphorisms; do not look for feel-good and no-stress and a lot-of-gain-and-no-pain kinds of books. They're all out there and you will be sorely tempted, but if you want to read something useful during these times, my brothers and sisters in Christ, read the letters of Paul. Read them and weep! Read them and rejoice! Read them and understand that neither you nor I are the first people in the world ever to face sorrow, death, frustration, or terror: we are not the first, and there is a record of coping here that is not merely of coping but of overcoming. If you do not wish to succumb to the tidal wave of despair and temptation and angst that surrounds us on every hand, you will go back to the roots of our faith, which are stronger than any form of patriotism. *I don't despise patriotism—don't misunderstand me—but there is no salvation in love of country. There is salvation only in love of Jesus Christ, and if you confuse the two, the greatest defeat will have been achieved.* Remember that. Read the letters of Paul.

When you look at that fourth chapter in 2 Corinthians, you will discover that this is not a faith of evasion, a faith of success, or a faith of unambiguous pleasure and delight. It is reality, a reality that believers have always been forced to face. "In the world," says the apostle John, "we shall have tribulation." Jesus says, "Be of good cheer; I have overcome the world." Well, that's all very right and good for Jesus, who in fact has overcome the world, and good for him, I say again; but for us who have not yet overcome the world, John's Gospel is as true as ever it was. In the world we shall have tribulation, and anyone who promises you otherwise is either uninformed or lying, and perhaps both; and owes no allegiance to the gospel. When we face the world as believers, we face it with tribulation on every hand.

From this very pulpit my venerable predecessor Willard Sperry often quoted his friend and colleague Georges Tyrell, who was one of the famous Catholic modernists of the first third of the twentieth century, and in a time when World War I was still fresh and World War II was clearly on the horizon, Sperry preached week after week to congregations like this— to your grandparents, three generations removed. One of his favorite quotations of Father Tyrell's was Tyrell's definition of Christianity, and this is what Tyrell said, what Sperry quoted, and what I now quote again: "Christianity is an ultimate optimism founded upon a provisional pessimism." In this world we shall have tribulation.

So, a reasonable person—and we're all reasonable persons here, are we not? That's why we're here and not in some other church—might ask, "From where has this notion come, that Christians are entitled to a free 'get-out-of-jail' card, an exemption to the world of turmoil and tribulation?" This misreading of the Christian faith (for that is exactly what it is) comes from the fashionable, cultural faith with which we have so often confused the Christian faith. Most of us aspire to be believers in the Christian faith, but all of us to one degree or another, alas, ascribe to the cultural faith. And that cultural religion in times of prosperity is often easy and always dangerous. Be suspicious of religion in times of prosperity and ease. Why is it dangerous? It is dangerous because prosperity itself can become a terribly tempting false god and a substitute for religion, and in the name of the religion of prosperity, success, and control, most of us will do anything and almost everything—and we have.

In times of prosperity either we make prosperity our religion, or we imagine that we can do without religion altogether. Who needs it? When turmoil happens to others we can be mildly empathetic, perhaps even sympathetic, and maybe we can even utter that famous aphorism, "There but for the grace of God go I"; but when turmoil hits us, when we are knocked flat, when all of our securities and our cherished illusions are challenged to the breaking point, and break, then comes the great question we must both ask and answer, "What is left when everything we have is taken from us?"

What is left when everything you have is taken from you? For the last decade I have asked on commencement morning, in my sermons to the seniors about to leave this college, questions like this: "How will you live after the fall?" I don't mean autumn; I mean the Fall. "How will you manage when trouble comes? How will you manage when you are tested and fail the test? How will you cope with frustration and fear and failure and anxiety?" Many of them have thought those to be quaint and even rude questions, perhaps the kind of rhetorical excess that preachers engage in around commencement time, a kind of raining on their parade.

Since September 11, however, these are no longer abstract, philosophical, or theoretical questions, and people have gravitated in astonishing numbers to the places where such questions are taken seriously. Every rabbi, minister, priest, imam, and spiritual leader of whom I know or have heard reports, as can I, the incredible turn toward faith in this time of our current crisis. Probably not since the Second World War has there been such a conspicuous turn to the faith in our country, and both our ordinary and our extraordinary services here in the last ten days bear profound witness to this. On Tuesday afternoon, September 11, the day of the terrorist attacks on the World Trade Center and the Pentagon, and the downing of the plane in Pennsylvania, we saw thousands here in the Yard in an ecumenical witness, and on Friday of that same week we saw almost as many here at a service of prayer and remembrance, on a day especially designated as a national day of prayer and remembrance. Last Sunday's service was like Easter day, and this one is very close to it. The daily service of morning prayers in Appleton Chapel is nearly standing-room only, and this past week the president of this university asked if he could come and speak at morning prayers on Friday, thus proving beyond all shadow of a doubt that there is a God. With his opening words from our lectern he said that this was the last place he expected to find himself so early in his administration. This is from a secular man who, by the standards of this secular place, is as close to God as many aspire to reach.

These are extraordinary times, this is an extraordinary moment, we are witnessing extraordinary things, and I ask you this: Is it not an incredible irony that in the face of the most terrible and tangible facts available to us, the destruction of those monuments to material success—the brutally physical, worldly reality with the violence before our very eyes—that men and women instinctively turn to the very things that cannot be seen? They turn not to the reality of the visible but to the reality of the invisible which, when compared to what can be seen, ultimately endures. Seeking faith amidst the ruins is the subtext of these days. There's a terrible parable there, that as the very temple to which we offered our secular worship is destroyed before us we seek the God who precedes and who follows these temples made and destroyed by human hands. People are seeking inner strength beyond the outer turmoil. That is what I see and that is what I hear on every hand, in every paper, in every magazine, on every talk show, and on everybody's lips.

In light of this, the question, "Where is God?" seems almost irrelevant. This was the question of the day for the religion editor of *The Boston Globe* last weekend, and a host of my clerical colleagues attempted an answer or two. I was not asked—another proof of the existence of God—but had I been, I would have said what I now say to you, which is that it was the wrong question. The question is not where God is when disaster strikes; the real and interesting question is where you were before disaster struck? Where were you two weeks ago? Three weeks ago? Where will you be three weeks from now, or four weeks from now? God has not forgotten you, but is it not reasonable to suggest that before September 11, many of us had forgotten God? God is where God always is and has always been; it is we who have to account for our absence.

Be certain of one thing, however. We should not be embarrassed that now in adversity we seek the God whom we had forgotten in prosperity, for what is God for if he is not to be there when we seek him? We should not be embarrassed that in trouble we have remembered one profound theological truth, that God is to be found where God is most needed—in trouble, sorrow, sickness, adversity, and even in death itself. Over and over and over again the psalms make this point, as we sang in the sermon hymn, in paraphrase of Psalm 46: "God is our refuge and strength; a very present help in trouble." Isn't this Luther's point in his great hymn "A Mighty Fortress Is Our God"?

> Let goods and kindred go,
> This mortal life also;
> The body they may kill;
> God's truth abideth still,
> His kingdom is forever.

You don't have to be a Lutheran to know the truth of that.

That hymn wasn't written yesterday. It was not written by someone who did not know turmoil. It was written by someone who in the midst of outer turmoil had inner strength.

This last week, as I've thought about this morning and my obligations toward you, two images have flashed in my mind. One was the indelible image of those burning towers and those terrible encounters with the airplanes, a kind of conflict of our own magnificent technologies coming together in a horrible parody of our skills and our strengths. That was one image. The other goes back to one of my favorite movies, which will identify all of my phobias and predilections and will also give away my age. Between Dunkirk and Pearl Harbor there was produced one great film, *Mrs. Miniver*. Those of you who know it know that I'm referring to that last scene in the bombed-out church on a Sunday morning, where, with the window destroyed and the cross standing in the broken window and the people of the congregation ripped apart by Hitler's bombing of their little village, yet still they sing, "Children of the heavenly King, as we journey sweetly sing." I know it was a great propaganda film. I know it was designed to rouse the souls and the spirits of the British people. I know it was the British version of Hollywood, with Walter Pigeon and Greer Garson. I know all of that, and I believe it! So did the British people, and so do you need to believe that in that destruction somewhere rests that image of the God who was with us at the most terrible moment of our time. The answer to the question, "Where is God?" is that God is where God is always—by the side of those who need him. He is not in front to lead, not behind to push, not above to protect, but beside us to get us through: "Beside us to guide us, our God with us joining."

I cannot imagine those heroic firefighters and police officers and workers and volunteers, amidst the rubble of Ground Zero in New York, indulging in the luxurious theological speculation about where God might or might not be. They *know* where God is; he is right there with them, enabling them, empowering them, strengthening them, even when hope itself has died. If you want to know where God is, do not ask the prosperous. Ask the suffering. Ask the sorrowing. Ask those who are acquainted with grief.

In the Book of Common Prayer there is a collect which begins, "God of all comfort..." To some who don't know any better, that sounds like mere consolation, something soothing, inadequate words in troubled times of turmoil and tribulation, a kind of Band-Aid on cancer, if you will, like the "comfortable words" in the old Book of Common Prayer, which were not very comforting to a church and a culture that had grown too comfortable. Do you know the proper meaning of the word "comfort"? It means to "fortify," to "strengthen," to "give courage," even "empower," and not mere consolation. The God of all comfort is the one who supplies what we most lack when we most need it. As Paul puts it, he gives us sufficient capacity that when we are knocked down we are not knocked out. The God of all comfort is not the god who fights like Superman or Rambo or Clint Eastwood or any of our conventional cultural heroes. The God of all comfort is the one who gives inner power and strength to those who would be easily outnumbered, outmaneuvered, outpowered by the conventional forces and the conventional wisdom. Inner strength is what is required when in the midst of turmoil we do not know what to do with our outward power and our outward might.

Let us also not forget one powerful fact that we are tempted to forget, which is that the world has always been a dangerous and precarious place. The fact that we have just discovered this terrible fact for ourselves does not make it any less true, or any less dangerous. Outer turmoil is no longer the fate that falls to others: the shrinking world that has allowed us to export technology abroad has now, alas, permitted terror to be imported to us. The great question now is how we stand and how we manage in a world now less brave, now less new than it ever was.

Inner strength, I believe, comes from the sure conviction that God has placed us in the world to do the work of life, and not of death. This is what Paul says in 2 Corinthians: "We are always facing death," he writes, "but this means that we know more and more of life" (2 Corinthians 4:11). Faith is not the opposite either of doubt or of death but the means whereby we face and endure doubt and death, and overcome our fear of them. Our inner faith as believers comes from the sure conviction that neither death nor doubt nor fear is the last word. This is not a policy statement for the nation; this is a sure conviction for Christian believers. Therefore, because we believe that, and because that belief is testified to by the experience of our ancestors in the faith and our contemporaries who labor beside us and for God in the rubble, we are able to endure. We are able to go through the worst for the best, come what may. Endurance is what it takes when you have nothing left. Phillips Brooks once said that we do not pray for lighter loads but for greater strength to bear the loads we are given. Heavy loads have been placed upon us in these days, and even greater burdens and sacrifices are to come: of that there can be no doubt. And, like Jesus in the garden, we would be less than human if we did not pray that this cup might pass us by—but it won't. The real issue for us then, as it was for Jesus, is, how do we manage?

Inner strength in the midst of turmoil, I suggest, is not simply stoic endurance and perseverance, important as they are, especially in tough, demanding times. Nor is inner strength simply a form of mind over matter, a kind of moral escapism that says that you may have captured my body but my mind is free. It's not only either of those. When I tried to think of what it was, I remembered a story told by old Dr. Ernest Gordon, for many years dean of the chapel at Princeton, who was more famous because of his book about his captivity on the River Kwai during World War II. In that Japanese prison camp, Ernest Gordon said that he and his fellow British who were captives were initially very religious, reading their Bibles, praying, singing hymns, witnessing, and testifying to their faith, and hoping and expecting that God would reward them and fortify them for their faith by freeing them or at least mitigating their captivity. God didn't deliver, however, and the men became both disillusioned and angry, and some even faithless. They gave up on the outward display of their faith, but after a while, Gordon says, the men, responding to the needs of their fellows—caring for them, protecting the weaker ones, and in some cases dying for one another—began to discern something of a spirit of God in their midst. It was not a revival of religion in the conventional sense, but rather the discovery that religion was not what you believed but what you did for others when it seemed that you could do nothing at all. It was compassion that gave them their inner strength, and it was from their inner strength that their compassion came. (I owe this insight to Dr. A. Leonard Griffiths, from *Illusions of our Culture*.)

Could it be that amidst the cries of vengeance and violence and warfare, and the turmoil that is attempting to sweep us all up in the calamity of these days, the inner strength we so desperately seek is the strength that comes from compassion, from hearing and heeding the cry of the other?

In one of Theodore Parker Ferris's books I found underlined these words about strength:

Some people's strength is all drawn from themselves. They are like isolated pools with limited reserves. Others are more like rivers. They do not produce or contain the power, but it flows through them, like blood through the body. The more they give, the more they are able to draw in. That strength is theirs, but it is not their own.

Then the author says, in words that I wish were mine:

The strength that God gives is available to those who care for others, for they are showing the spirit of Jesus. The power of God's spirit fortifies them.[1]

Can it be that inner strength is not simply the capacity to endur, but to give? Can it be that compassion is superior to power? Can it be that amid the turmoil of that violent crowd on Good Friday, from his inner strength Jesus showed compassion? He forgave his enemies, he reunited his friends, and he redeemed the criminal.

When in the midst of turmoil and calamity you seek the inner strength that helps you not only to endure but to overcome, do not look for what you can get. Look rather for what you have been given, and for what you can give. We begin with calamity, but we end with compassion. Remember the quotation that Theodore Ferris had underlined: "The strength that God gives is available for those who care for others...."

---

[1]Hugh Martin. *The Beatitudes* (New York: Harper & Brothers, 1953).

Annihilation, Retaliation, Reconciliation, and the Pursuit of Justice: An Ethical Reflection

Richard W. Wills Sr.

SEPTEMBER 29, 2001

S eptember 11, 2001 created a category for catastrophe unlike any that we have ever witnessed on American soil. The sense of not knowing what meaning to assign to so heavy a tragedy caused some to posit a "we'll understand it better by and by" conception of the tragedy. And yet every conscientious wrestler of life's weighty questions is compelled to think and speak about human tragedy in the "now" so as to minimize its cause and effect in the "future." A future anticipating that justice inevitably will overcome.

Within the discipline of ethics, one can locate ethical frameworks that assist our thinking about how annihilation, retaliation, and reconciliation relate to the question of justice, and to what extent the means we choose impact the ways in which justice is realized and sustained. In seeking to envision the relationship between the various means that are available in one's pursuit of justice, and the process by which we arrive at a specific means, I have located annihilation and reconciliation in positions juxtaposed to one another, with retaliation centered between the tension created by these two seemingly polar opposite experiences.

In response to an injustice, individuals within a democracy, both religious and nonreligious, may mediate between their understanding of the "rule of law" and the "law of love" as guides to their conscience. While each response located within the spectrum of possibilities may be viewed as a socially viable means toward the realization of justice, one must fundamentally ask, *What type of a climate is created given the means used to realize justice, and is a more ideal means of realizing justice available to human beings in search of being more humane?*

Recognizing the brevity of this essay and the length to which we could compare and contrast concepts of justice, I shall narrow my definition of justice to that of Martin Luther King Jr.'s because of his universal acclaim as an advocate of justice and peace and the experiential similarities that exist between the context out of which he wrote and that out of which we currently write and reflect.

King, as in the case of Paul Tillich, essentially affirmed that, "creative justice is the form of reuniting love,"[1] the instrument that love assumes in reuniting that which is separated and estranged. Justice is transformed into a type of propelling potency by love for the purpose of reconciling ruptured relations. In this regard, King saw the affirmation of justice as that which was wholly compatible and entirely in harmony with the principles of God's love. Justice was not simply viewed as a negation of evil but as an occasion for both the oppressed and the oppressor to experience a type of liberation that would ultimately result in the reconciliation of society.

In this sense King's concept of justice represented love's (*agape*) attempt to reunite the disconnected elements of life into a harmonious whole and thus hasten the realization of a *Beloved Community.*[2] As did King, I say that there is a reality beyond annihilation and retaliation that merits our serious consideration, namely the way of reconciliation!

Though his ethical analysis was far from exhaustive and vulnerable to critique, it did begin to approach and move us toward a new understanding of what justice *could* look like, how it *could* be achieved and why it *could* be pursued in a manner that encourages reconciliation. Admittedly, his ethical viewpoint was defined, and perhaps even narrowed, by specific cultural values and theological symbols, as is ours. And yet if all truth is God's truth, something of what he saw, and what we hope to see in our modern era, ought to approximate some degree of universal accessibility and understanding.

For the ethicist, the way one pursues justice is as critical as justice realized.

There is a correlation between the means we choose and the kind of social climate our means create, which is why retaliation, even in the instance of a just war, is generally considered a last resort.

Even with carefully planned and deployed acts of retaliation, one runs the risk of never freeing oneself from the *cycle* of physical force as normative in future pursuits of justice. Aggression creates a climate conducive to continued acts of counter aggression. War becomes the primary deterrence to war. To this, one might respond that it is not the act of annihilation or retaliation, but the reality of evil in the world that creates and establishes the parameters limiting our capacity to respond non-aggressively. The ethical question, however, that this conception of justice raises is, can a response other than annihilation or retaliation sufficiently curb the force of evil, so as to move our response to something more akin to reconciliation, thereby creating a global climate more conducive to a universal conception of justice?

One can scarcely know whether or not a more ideal means of realizing justice is available to human beings in search of being more humane unless the possibilities for that reality are presented and reasoned through. In a democracy, questions of this sort are raised and scrutinized in what is termed, by ethicists and others, the public square.

Within the public square dialogue, an absolute pacifist could argue that nothing short of reconciliation can achieve lasting justice, while a non-pacifist position might want to assess each situation individually and insist that one must weigh the response chosen from the broad range of possibilities against a given act of violence so as to avoid social irresponsibility.

As the options are weighed one would ask, "Is the willingness to participate in constructive discourse about peace a shared desire? Is the language mutually accessible? Is there a willingness to compromise in the event of non-consensus? Is the climate mutually conducive to notions of reconciliation versus retaliation of one sort or another?" A conversation along these lines could conclude that retaliation as a means toward justice should be exercised only in support of a "just war," a war that is waged to defend the victims of horrific, sustained, reckless aggression, or to secure freedom for the abjectly oppressed.

Ideally the intent of a public square would be to provide a venue for discourse that is responsive to the range of possibilities that broaden as the international affirmation of some form of democratic dialogue broadens. This sort of dialogical transformation is both possible and necessary in an ever shrinking world-house.

The marvelous reality is that within the context of a just democracy this kind of open discourse in which ethical, theological, and political ideas are debated with hopes of creating an overlapping consensus, is encouraged. At our best, this is the kind of discourse that has set our nation apart from other less tolerable regimes, a dialogical process through which the public and its officials arrive at an understanding of what is in the best interest.

Retaliation may be presented as the ethically correct solution to acts of violence in the world, but democratic process requires that the accepted response represent the byproduct of a truly informed public consensus. Through this process of consensus in support of one response over another, a societal intersection is defined in which sacred and secular values discover common ground based on common cultural and historical realities.

Heightened security is an absolute must on the heels of the violence leveled against this nation. No rational being would argue that fact. The fear is that in this heightened state of alarm, we neglect to remember that which makes us distinctly American, our love for freedom and our respect and regard for the other, even when the other holds opinions that may differ from that of our own.

Short of this mutual regard, dialogue is reduced to provincial monologue so that ideas such as those put forth by King in the public square begin to sound foreign, is ignored by removing it from the circles of serious discourse and relegating it to the fringe, or worse yet is severely criticized and threatened for failing to comply with the larger populace. If in fact justice has more to do with reconciliation than it has to do with revenge, how do we get to a place where that reality of reconciliation seems plausible apart from an ongoing open discourse about what is possible? We must will it, work untiringly for it and be prepared to wait untiringly for its arrival. We must pray for it, vote for it and live as its personification.

Despite the militant call to retaliation during his day, King insisted upon reconciliation as the normative road toward justice. Much more than the eloquent theorist, King became a practitioner of peace and an ambassador of nonviolence. As such he determined to demonstrate the credibility of his ethical conception in the trenches of life. One can scarcely imagine how King and other Americans of African descent, along with others of good will from every race and creed, lived with the daily dread and fear that must have exceeded that of our current experience. Theirs was a daily experience of not knowing when, or fully understanding why the next attack would come. Less than fifty years ago, parsonages were bombed, churches were destroyed. In Montgomery during the bus boycotts, parents nightly placed their children in bathtubs, not beds, for safe keeping. Unarmed persons bowed in prayer were assaulted. Human life was terrorized, and innocent children were murdered in church on Sunday morning, not at the hands of foreign zealots, but by fellow citizens of our great democracy.

The counsel offered to parents of fear-ridden children was found in the assurance that although "the arc of the universe is long, it is bent toward justice." And it was in this confidence that King's ethical conviction remained intact and undeterred. Under no circumstance would violence against the perpetuators of violence be deemed a valid alternative in the procurement of lasting justice. Martin Luther King Jr. conceived an ethic that pursued justice via the ways of reconciliation, not revenge.

As a result of this moral compass provided for us toward the close of the twentieth century, countless lives of every race, gender, creed, and nation have become the beneficiaries of the civil rights movement's efforts. In light of our current climate, one cannot help but wonder what type of compass we are providing for those who shall come along in the shadow of our passing?

Tragedy has a way of surfacing the best and worst tendencies within the human condition, and we have certainly seen suggestions of both since September eleventh. The essential goodness and resiliency of the human spirit is being reaffirmed by our capacity to empathize with the irreparable loss of others, but we are also witnessing a rise in racial intolerance, a slow but steady diminishing of civil liberty, a heightened sense of irrational fear and suspicion, in addition to the sharp narrowing of what is deemed acceptable rhetoric. What will we gain and what will we forfeit in this pursuit of justice? It will depend upon our means.

On December 10, 1964 Martin Luther King Jr. traveled with family and close associates to Oslo, Norway, to accept the Nobel Peace Prize. His acceptance speech was a moving affirmation that celebrated the hope of human existence beyond the threat of human extinction. Beyond whining bullets, mortar bursts, and blood-stained streets, King envisioned the ushering in of a day that would be safeguarded by an equitable distribution of food, the provision of cultural and educational excellence, and a far greater realization of global freedom and human dignity. It was a speech that affirmed the creation of an international community with the capacity to curb violence without the exercise of violence. Resolute in his conviction, King stated his refusal to accept the idea of thermonuclear destruction as an inevitable reality. For him, the agents of unarmed truth and unconditional love would have the final word. As such, the Nobel Peace Prize was accepted with the belief that a growing culture of global good will would ultimately overcome.[2]

The question one must ask oneself in the wake of the eleventh is "How will justice overcome now?" I suggest that creative justice will overcome now as it has overcome in the past, through the tireless and courageous efforts of human beings in search of being more humane. Simply stated, the advocates of reconciliation will have to remain as committed to building a global community as the advocates of violence are to tearing it down.

This undoubtedly is a military war that we can win. And yet, in the final analysis, when inventory has been taken, it may not be whom we have found in the hill country of Afghanistan that decides the difference, but what we may have lost as a nation in the process of raiding and bombing instead of listening and engaging, that ultimately determines whether we have won or lost this war.

---

[1] Paul Tillich, *Love, Power and Justice* (New York: Oxford University Press, 1954), 66.
[2] Martin Luther King Jr., *Where Do We Go From Here: Chaos or Community?* (Boston: Beacon Press, 1967), 171.

A Pastoral Prayer for a National Tragedy

J. Alfred Smith Sr.

September 16, 2001

This prayer was prayed at the Allen Temple Baptist Church, Oakland, California, where Congresswoman Barbara Lee is a member. Congresswoman Lee was the only member of the Senate to vote against granting the president $40 billion for war after the September 11, 2001 attack on the Word Trade Center and the Pentagon.

O God and Creator of humankind,
O God of Muslim, Christian, and Jew,
O God of agnostic skepticism and atheistic unbelief,
O God of the prince and the pauper, the poet and the peasant,
the powerful and the powerless, the prosperous and the poor,
forgive our foolish ways.
Reclothe us in our right minds,
that we too may find the precious truth of Congresswoman Barbara Lee,
that we cannot put out the hellish fire of destruction and death
with the mighty firepower of missiles and munitions.
Distill from our circulatory system the venom of hatred.
Take away the horns of nations
and replace them with halos of harmony.

We seek your blessing for grieving families
fractured, fragile, and frustrated
by the senseless sinfulness of evil highjackers
who in the name of religion kill American citizens
with American-taught knowledge.
We seek your blessing for orphaned children, who are scarred for life
because of killers infected with the mania of murder,
for every firefighter and for every police officer (living and dead)
who went beyond the call of duty to save lives,
for heroic volunteers who are still helping as angels of mercy,
for heavenly wisdom that will guide the president and his advisors
in meeting this earthly crisis,
and for the rest of us, frozen with the ice of psychic and emotional pain.

Chase away the ugly clouds of despair
and place the smiling sun back into the sky,
so that once again our days will be bright and beautiful.
Save us from the hard times of an economic recession.
Place steel in our spines, so that we will stand with dignity.
Give us the appetite to hunger and thirst after righteousness.

Help the churches, synagogues, and mosques to teach our society
that we cannot be blessed with answered prayers
if we harbor hate and nourish revenge for our enemies.
This is our prayer that we pray in the name of Jesus Christ,
the crucified one, who was a man of sorrows acquainted with grief,
and who is our wounded healer. Amen.

Afterword
In Times Like These, Deliver Us from Evil

Frank A. Thomas

P hillipe Halsman was the photographer who took the legendary photograph of Albert Einstein that has been displayed worldwide and was featured on the cover of the December 1999, *Time* magazine. Halsman asked Einstein, as he released the camera's shutter, "So you don't believe there will ever be peace?" Halsman recalls, "Einstein's eyes had a look of immense sadness as well as a question and a reproach." He answered, "No, as long as there will be man, there will be war."[1] When the airplanes hit the Twin Towers of the World Trade Center on September 11, 2001, I knew in the deep levels of my soul that Einstein was correct. In this world, as long as human beings exist, there will be war.

War has been with us from the beginning and will be with us until the end of time. War is the human endeavor that has been waged on every continent and among every people. War rivals sex as the primary force for the movement and distribution of people and resources on the planet. War seems to erupt naturally wherever human beings are found. Even sacred texts such as the Old Testament regularly celebrate war. For example, Joshua succeeded Moses and led the Israelites to conquer (i.e., kill all the people and take their land) more than thirty kingdoms whose territory the Israelites called the "Promised Land." War, violence, and genocide is one of the central activities of the Old Testament. Raymond Schwager points out that there a hundred passages where Yahweh expressly commands human beings to kill other people, and several stories where God tries to kill for no apparent reason (e.g., Exodus 4:24-26).[2] René Girard understands the Old Testament as a "long and laborious exodus out of the world of violence and sacred projections, an exodus plagued by many reversals and falling short of its goal."[3] The New Testament, centered in the resurrection of Jesus Christ, inaugurates the kingdom of God, a new order of human behavior that does not use violence to resolve human conflict and does not project human violence onto God. But despite the inauguration of the kingdom of God, the consummation of the kingdom will only occur after the final war between good and evil, God and Satan, contained in Revelation 20. After reading the Revelation text, I am even more convinced that "as long as there is man there will be war."

But despite the longevity and universality of war, we have a hard time agreeing on a definition of war. War has been called everything from a "great adventure" to "hell on earth." Prussian military genius Carl Von Clauswitz insisted that "War is merely the continuation of policy by other means." In contrast, a popular song of the 1970s rhetorically asked and answered the question of war: "War! What is it good for? Absolutely nothing!"

By way of clarification, it is important to establish a definition of war. Michael Ghiglieri says, "War is conflict between social groups that is resolved by individuals on one or both sides killing those of the opposite side."[4] The ethical dimensions of war can be defined by, but not limited to, four basic modes of thought: (1) unjust or offensive war: consists of and is defined by the intention to steal en mass what another group owns and to leave members of that group dead; (2) just war or self-defense: the effort and intent to defend and keep another group from stealing what you own and leaving you dead; (3) pacifism and non-violence: assumes that all war is unjust and only leads to continuing cycles of retaliatory violence and idiocy that will ultimately descend into nuclear disintegration; (4) holy war or crusade: waged in the name of God to totally exterminate and subjugate "infidels" and "nonbelievers." The American government, the majority of the American public, and many nations of the world define the attack of September 11 as an act of offensive war and provocation.

Our response is a just war of self-defense. America is at war, as President Bush says, "to protect freedom, democracy, and our way of life."

My concern is that evil tends to mask itself in the cloak of war. Some of the most gruesome, inhumane, and despicable acts known to humankind have been perpetrated under the guise and justification of war, often in the name of God. Can we truly distinguish war from the evil that so often disguises itself in the clothing of war? Or, is war inherently evil so that every time we go to war, we are engaging in an evil act? Or, must we go to war to stop the march of evil? As I think about September 11 and our response of war, the words of Jesus in Matthew 6:13, in the midst of what is commonly known as the Lord's Prayer, ring vividly in my soul: "Deliver us from evil (the evil one)."

Jesus understood the true power, nature, size, scope, depth, reality, and impact of evil. Jesus understood that evil is so despicable, so desperate, so depraved, so destructive, so vicious, and so able to bring death, misery, and pain that he simply prayed that we would be delivered from it. Jesus understood that evil fundamentally does not make sense. How does one make sense of evil? What is the rhyme and reason, the rationale and thinking behind evil? What sense does evil make? Jesus knew better than anybody ever has or ever will that evil makes no sense at all.

Evil is tearing up for the hell of it, killing people for the hell of it, destroying the fabric of lives, families, and nations for the hell of it. "For the hell of it" means for no purpose, with no sustainable result in mind and no end that can be justified. Evil destroys and tears up for the hell of it. Evil runs airplanes into buildings, but evil can also bomb an already tragic country. Evil has many faces; terrorism might be one and patriotism can be another. Evil can lurk not only in the Taliban and Osama bin Laden, but also in President Bush and the U.S. Congress. Evil can show up in any country, at any time, strike in any party or government. Evil can be personal evil where a child is raped or abused, or evil can be structural where an entire people are given "Bantu" education and have their futures limited, if not cut off. Evil can center in individual people, such as Hitler, and in entire social institutions, such as courts, police, banks, schools, and churches, as in the case of the American sanctioning of the slave trade, apartheid, Jim Crow, and the genocide of Rwanda. Evil has so many faces that, essentially, evil is faceless. Jesus was so aware of the devastating power of evil that he prayed in the Lord's Prayer that we would be delivered from evil. Deliver us from evil.

This prayer of Jesus recognizes several painful realities, realities which have been illustrated all too painfully through the attack on September 11. First, we ask God to deliver us from evil because, however well planned and organized human resources are, those resources are inadequate to deal with evil and with all the eventualities, possibilities, and circumstances of evil. This is not to say that we should not establish security checkpoints, gather intelligence, screen luggage, and do absolutely everything at our human disposal to protect our safety. But we must recognize that our resources cannot prepare for every eventuality. This prayer recognizes a weakness and destructiveness in the world that can be only defined as evil.

This leads to the second painful reality with which we must come to terms. Jesus prayed "Deliver us from evil" realizing that not everyone *will* be delivered in this sphere of human existence. Many died in the collapsing structure and debris of the World Trade Center, in the wreckage of the crashed airliner near Pittsburgh, in the fiery heat of the burning Pentagon. Some die from state-sponsored terrorism, ethnic cleansing, and genocide. Some die at the hands of a drive-by shooter. Whole nations of Native American people died as colonists and pioneers waged an offensive holy war for this land. Children are molested and people are raped, and their traumatized spirits die. Martin Luther King Jr. died in Memphis from an assassin's bullet. Not all of us will escape the tentacles and the clutches of evil. It is not possible for all of us to be delivered from the desperate and despicable acts of evil.

If we are not careful, these painful realities will lead us to fear the future. When Jesus prayed "Deliver us from evil," he suggested that we could not get around the fact that the future is uncertain, and therefore living becomes an act of faith, not of planning, an act of trust and not of control.[5] This does not mean that we should not plan, but we must place our plans in the hands of the One who can deliver us from evil.

This kind of prayerful living is further complicated by the fact that we must not only be concerned with being victims of evil, but we must also watch the ways with which we can so easily further the "destructive and uncreative aims of evil." If we are not careful, we will too easily cooperate with evil. If we will not actively perpetrate evil, our silence and acquiescence can help evil to flourish. Our patriotism, nationalism, technology, and military and economic superiority can be instruments of evil. President Bush, with all this capability at his disposal, needs to be prayed for. I ask God to deliver him and his cabinet from evil. This is what we mean we pray "Deliver us from evil": we do not want to perpetrate evil or have evil perpetrated upon us.

In all of the stark reality latent in this phrase from the Lord's Prayer, there is also a word of tremendous hope. Jesus would not teach us to ask for deliverance if deliverance were not available. Deliverance *is* available. Evil can do its worst, but deliverance is available. No matter what evil does, evil will not have the last word. Jesus suffered crucifixion at the hands of evil. Jesus was buried in a borrowed tomb at the hands of evil. But the resurrection is the guarantor that evil will not win, that death will have not the victory. The resurrection is the guarantee that we will not be overcome.

Planes will run into buildings and thousands will die, but we will not be overcome. Wars will ravage the landscape of our world, but we will not be overcome. We might be raped and molested, but we will not be overcome. The poet said, "The wheels of justice grind slowly, but they grind exceedingly fine." We shall not be overcome. A lie cannot live forever, and truth crushed to the earth will rise again. We shall not be overcome. The Bible says, "You shall reap what you sow." We shall not be overcome. We can take courage that right defeated is more powerful than evil triumphant. We shall not be overcome. Jesus can give us the assurance that evil will not have the last word because evil did not have the last word with him.

Julian of Norwich, the great English mystic, in *Revelation of Divine Love* says, "Thou shalt not be overcome, was said . . . for sureness and comfort against all tribulation which may come. He said not, 'Thou shalt not be troubled. Thou shalt not be travailed. Thou shalt not be distressed.' But he said, 'Thou shall not be overcome.'" Einstein was correct: "As long as there is man, there will be war." But God will deliver us from evil and we will not be overcome.

[1] *Time*, 31 December 1999.

[2] Raymond Schwager, *Must There Be Scapegoats?* (San Francisco: Harper & Row, 1987), 46-67, 119.

[3] René Girard, *Violence and the Sacred* (Baltimore: John Hopkins University Press, 1977).

[4] Michael P. Ghiglieri, *The Dark Side of Man: Tracing the Origins of Male Violence* (Cambridge, Mass.: Perseus Books, 1999), 160.

[5] Kenneth Stevenson, *Abba Father: Understanding and Using the Lord's Prayer* (Harrisburg: Morehouse Publishing, 2000), 111.

Contributors

CHARLES G. ADAMS is pastor of Hartford Memorial Baptist Church in Detroit, Michigan, and past president of the Progressive National Baptist Convention. He is among the deans of African American clergy, an archetype of classic black preaching.

CHARLES E. BOOTH is pastor of Mount Olivet Baptist Church in Columbus, Ohio. He is one of the most renowned revivalists of the past quarter century and is also a member of the advisory board of *The African American Pulpit*.

GAIL E. BOWMAN is the chaplain at Dillard University in New Orleans, Louisiana. She is also the author of *Praying the Sacred in Secular Settings*.

CALVIN O. BUTTS III is pastor of the historic Abyssinian Baptist Church in Harlem, New York. He was among the clergy who addressed the nation from Shea Stadium in New York following the tragedy of September 11, 2001.

DELORES CARPENTER is professor of religious education at Howard University School of Divinity in Washington, D.C., and pastor of Michigan Park Christian Church. Her most recent publications include serving as general editor for *The African American Heritage Hymnal*.

MICHAEL ERIC DYSON, Ph.D., is the Ida B. Wells Barnett University Professor at De Paul University in Chicago, Illinois. He is author of *Between God and Gansta Rap* and most recently, *I May Not Get There with You: The True Martin Luther King Jr.*

CAIN HOPE FELDER, Ph.D., is chair of the Biblical Institute for Social Change, Inc., and professor of New Testament studies at Howard University School of Divinity in Washington, D.C. He is also the author of numerous books, including *Troubling Biblical Waters*, and editor of *The Original African Heritage Study Bible*.

ROBERT M. FRANKLIN is president of the Interdenominational Theological Center in Atlanta, Georgia, and a senior fellow at Emory University's Center for the Interdisciplinary Study of Religion. His publications include *Another Day's Journey: Black Churches Confronting the American Crisis*.

PETER J. GOMES is Plummer Professor of Christian Morals and Pusey Minister in The Memorial Church at Harvard University in Cambridge, Massachusetts. His books include *The Good Book: Reading the Bible with Mind and Heart*.

JESSE LOUIS JACKSON SR. is president of The Rainbow Coalition. In 1984 he was a candidate for the presidency of the United States. He was a recipient of the Presidential Medal of Freedom in 2000.

T. D. JAKES is pastor of The Potter's House in Dallas, Texas, and is prominent for his television ministry. He is the author of numerous publications, including the bestseller *Woman, Thou Art Loosed!*

CAROLYN ANN KNIGHT is assistant professor of homiletics at the Interdenominational Theological Center in Atlanta, Georgia, and a member of the advisory board of *The African American Pulpit.*

VASHTI MURPHY McKENZIE is the first woman bishop of the African Methodist Episcopal Church and a member of the advisory board of *The African American Pulpit.* She is the author of several books; her most recent publication is *Strength in the Struggle: Leadership Development for Women.*

J ALFRED SMITH SR. is pastor of Allen Temple Baptist Church, professor of preaching at the American Baptist Seminary of the West, Berkeley, California, and a past president of the Progressive National Baptist Convention. His numerous books include *Falling in Love with God* and *No Other Help I Know.*

GARDNER C. TAYLOR has been one of the best known and most admired clergy in America for more than half a century. He is pastor emeritus of Concord Baptist Church in Brooklyn, New York, an advisory board member of *The African American Pulpit,* and a recipient of the Presidential Medal of Freedom in 2000.

WALTER S. THOMAS is pastor of New Psalmist Baptist Church in Baltimore, Maryland, and president of the Hampton University Ministers' Conference and Choir Directors and Organists Guild Workshop. He is also author of several books, including *Good Meat Makes Its Own Gravy* and *Spiritual Navigation for the 21st Century,* both published by Judson Press.

WILLIAM D. WATLEY is pastor of St. James African Methodist Episcopal Church in Newark, New Jersey, and a member of the advisory board of *The African American Pulpit.* He is also author of several books, including *From Mess to Miracle,* and coauthor of *The African Presence in the Bible,* both published by Judson Press.

RICHARD W. WILLS SR. formerly served as pastor at Dexter Avenue King Memorial Baptist Church in Montgomery, Alabama, during which time he coedited the book *Reflections on Our Pastor: Dr. Martin Luther King Jr. at Dexter Avenue Baptist Church, 1954-1960.* Currently he is pastor of Pilgrim Baptist Church in Virginia.

JEREMIAH A. WRIGHT JR. is pastor of Trinity United Church of Christ in Chicago, Illinois. An advisory board member of *The African American Pulpit,* he is also the author of *What Makes You So Strong?* and *Good News!,* both published by Judson Press.

Excavators at Ground Zero unearthed from the wreckage a steel girder that formed a cross. They erected it as a memorial atop the rubble of the Twin Towers, a powerful symbol of resurrection in the midst of the devastation and destruction of September 11, 2001. Here, rescue workers and excavators stand as prayerful witnesses while a priest blesses the steel monument of remembrance.